COMMUNICATION BEFORE SPEECH

Normal Development and Impaired Communication

Edited by
JUDITH COUPE and JULIET GOLDBART

CROOM HELM
London • New York • Sydney

© 1988 Judith Coupe and Juliet Goldbart
Croom Helm Ltd, Provident House, Burrell Row,
Beckenham, Kent BR3 1AT

Croom Helm Australia, 44-50 Waterloo Road,
North Ryde, 2113, New South Wales

Published in the USA by
Croom Helm
in association with Methuen, Inc.
29 West 35th Street
New York, NY 10001

British Library Cataloguing in Publication Data

Communication before speech: normal
   development and impaired communication.
      1. Interpersonal communication in children
      I. Coupe, Judith II. Goldbart, Juliet
      155.4′13   BF723.C57
   ISBN 0-7099-4841-7
   ISBN 0-7099-4848-4 Pbk

Library of Congress Cataloging-in-Publication Data

Communication before speech: normal development and impaired
   communication/edited by Judith Coupe and Juliet Goldbart.
      p. cm.
   Bibliography: p.
   Includes index.
   ISBN 0-7099-4841-7. ISBN 0-7099-4848-4 (pbk.)
      1. Communicative disorders in children — Patients — Language.
   2. Language acquisition. I. Coupe, Judith D. II. Goldbart,
   Juliet.
   RJ496.C67C66   1987
   155.4′13 — dc19   87-23052

Typeset by Leaper & Gard Ltd, Bristol, England
Printed and bound in Great Britain
by Billings & Sons Limited, Worcester.

Contents

Acknowledgements

Our thanks go to our colleagues, especially to the pupils and staff of Melland School who have been a source of inspiration. Particular thanks are due to Ann Fitzmaurice for her unstinting support and time, and to Peter Mittler, Judy Sebba, Helen McConachie, Jenny May, Jill Porter and Liz Collins for their commitment to the BIMH conferences from which this book emerged.

This book is dedicated to our parents,
Frank, Doreen, Carole and Colin,
and to the many children we have taught
and will go on to teach.

Contributors

Mark Barber: teacher at Melland School, for pupils with severe learning difficulties. His main interests and expertise concern students with complex problems of social and emotional adjustment and also the development of early cognition and communication.

Linda Barton: formerly Senior Speech Therapist, South Manchester Health Authority, is now working with pre-school children for the Department of Speech Therapy, Auckland, New Zealand. She has a particular interest in the development of pragmatics, early communication and cognition.

Judith Coupe: Head Teacher of Melland School, previously worked on a Schools Council project with the Hester Adrian Research Centre and was an Advisory Teacher for Cheshire L.E.A. She is concerned with all areas of curriculum development, in particular with ways of facilitating pupils' strategies for acting on and communicating about the environment.

Juliet Goldbart, Ph.D: is a Lecturer in Psychology in the Department of Psychology and Speech Pathology at Manchester Polytechnic. She is currently engaged in research on early interactions, communication and cognition. She is particularly concerned with methods for increasing severely and profoundly handicapped students' opportunities for affecting their environments.

Jane Jolliffe: is a Senior Speech Therapist with Central Manchester Health Authority. Her full-time commitment is to the development of communicative competence in children and adults with severe learning difficulties.

Chris Kiernan, Ph.D: is Professor of Behavioural Studies in Mental Handicap and Director of Hester Adrian Research Centre, University of Manchester. Formerly Deputy Director of the Thomas Coram Research Unit, University of London Institute of Education. Main interests: the analysis and remediation of severe communication problems and problem behaviours in people with mental handicap, with particular reference to problems of integration within community settings.

Debbie Murphy: is a teacher at Melland School whose particular expertise lies in the education of children with profound and multiple impairments. She has recently completed an additional qualification as a teacher of the hearing impaired at the University of Manchester.

Sue Walker: formerly a mainstream teacher in music is now at Melland School. She is a specialist in expressive arts and is involved in developing reasoning and problem-solving strategies for developmentally young pupils both in her class and throughout the school.

Foreword

Peter Mittler
Professor of Special Education University of Manchester

Out of every 100 children in schools for children with severe learning difficulties, 25 have not yet started to use single words. The utterances of half the children are unintelligible to their teachers.

These figures come from surveys carried out on several thousand children ten years ago (Leeming et al, 1979; Mittler and Preddy, 1981). But would the results be very different today? On the one hand, we have learned a great deal about early language and communication. Teachers and speech therapists have themselves contributed to this knowledge and are better trained and more confident. They have also responded to the challenge presented by these children by introducing signing and other non-verbal systems on a large scale. On the other hand, it seems that the population in the schools may have more severe impairments than ten years ago. Some of the abler children are attending other special schools and a few are in ordinary schools with varying degrees of support. Hospital schools, which previously admitted some of the children with the most severe and multiple impairments, are almost all now closed.

This book reminds us that we must also meet the challenge posed by adults with communication impairments. For the past ten years, an increasing number of young people who would previously have been admitted for permanent hospital care have been retained in the care of community services. People in hospitals are beginning to be relocated to community services. What provision is being made for adults with severe communication problems in adult training centres, further education colleges and other community services (McCartney, 1984)? How can we ensure that there is continuity of teaching from school to adult services? What working links have been developed between school and adult training centre staff? What are the implications of the new Disabled Persons Act, 1986, which calls for the equivalent of a statement of need and a commitment to provision? Are we making enough use of the new microelectronic technology and do people with intellectual disabilities get access to the same level of professional support, aids and appliances as those with physical disabilities? What access do staff working with adults with mental handicap have to courses and workshops to update their knowledge and skills?

Professionals, policy makers and parents are now confronting the challenge of designing and delivering a curriculum for individuals of all ages whose levels of communicative or cognitive development may appear to be no higher than a few weeks. The cognitive ability of children with limited communication is easily underestimated, resulting in even lower levels of demand and expectation. Assessing children with severely limited experiences on developmental checklists can result in further underestimation. Obstacles to their development are thus formidable and in some respects immovable. Quite apart from the impairments of the children themselves, we have to confront the barrier of our own and others' underestimation of their ability to learn. Faced with people with such severe impairments, it is not surprising that teachers and parents should sometimes become discouraged by their apparent failure to develop or begin to wonder whether their efforts are really worth while — particularly with adults. It is all too easy to accept poorer levels of staffing and services on the grounds that these individuals have reached a 'plateau' and will not develop further.

The authors of this book provide ample evidence that the challenge is at least beginning to be met. Teachers and speech therapists are finding new insights in the way language and communication normally develop. This knowledge is now being re-examined in the light of the needs of children whose development is severely impaired from whatever cause. As a result, we have a better idea of the principles underlying a communication curriculum, though we still have far to go in translating this knowledge into successful outcomes for children.

The lessons learned from a study of normal development are not strikingly new and may at first seem obvious. But it is only recently that we have begun to incorporate them into day-to-day work with children. We are now more aware of the nature and quality of the day-to-day interactions between adults and children and between children themselves. Even in a well-run and lively school, children may have remarkably little direct, one-to-one interaction with an adult, other than for routine activities. How many of these interactions, whether verbal or non-verbal, are initiated by the child? Who responds and how? What happens as a result? How often do we provide each child with opportunities for choice and decision making? How can we help a child to learn that initiations of interaction are rewarding and lead to desired outcomes? Are there dangers in a well-run school such that we might unwittingly deprive a child of such opportunities? Can individual educational programmes allow children to affect, or even control, the structure of the day? In our concern with reaching objectives, have we left space for children to influence their own curriculum?

All the contributors to this book stress that communication can only be understood and taught in the social context of inter-actions with others. The demands we make of children, the expectations we have of their capacity to understand and respond and our interpretation of their response are all affected by the history of our own experiences with the child in front of us. The roots of communication lie in the first relationships we make — in the first smile, even the first reflex grasp of the newborn baby's finger. Research over the past decade has shown rich and regular patterns of social communication between adults and babies, with clear evidence of turn-taking and synchronisation in communication even in the first few weeks. Earlier research had shown that babies as young as this were much more advanced than had been thought in their ability to make fine perceptual discriminations and even to express choice and preference for one kind of sensory input than another and that they were able to learn from their experience (Bower, 1974).

What can we learn from such research? First, we can take comfort from the fact that only a small number of children with severe learning difficulties are functioning at the developmental level of a baby of only a few weeks of age, and that even at this level there is evidence of some ability to discriminate and to learn. Second, research on infants with cognitive or communi-cative impairments has suggested that although similar patterns of behaviour and interaction can be observed, such children are often much slower in their reactions. A baby with Down's syndrome may take much longer to return the adult's smile or cooing. But we should not be discouraged by an apparent lack of response or attribute this to the baby's impairments — we must simply wait a few seconds longer for a response (Cunningham and Sloper, 1978). A third recurrent theme concerns the importance of arranging the environment so that the child has something to communicate *about*. This book reports a number of ways in which we can fail or succeed in this. For instance, how many of our language interactions with children are sterile requests for information that we already know?

This book reports simple but ingenious examples of putting the onus of communication on the child — pencils that need sharpening, milk that is not where it should be, scissors that won't cut, light switches that don't work, a toy just out of reach. One recalls Gunzburg's suggestion some 25 years ago that hospitals for people with mental handicap should represent an obstacle course to provide learning experiences akin to those that are found in the 'real world'. How often do we arrange the learning environment in such a way as to make life as consistent and predictable as possible? How little is left to chance in our schools? Are we in danger of over-programming?

Arising from this is the rediscovery of the principle that teaching has to take place in the natural environment and in the context of ordinary, day-to-day needs and encounters — in shops, on public transport and in the street. Language teaching is therefore less concerned with one-to-one sessions in a quiet corner of the classroom or living-room, but should involve instead a conscious widening of the child's interactions and experiences with the aim of creating situations of demand and expectation. A further justification for such an approach arises from the problems children with severe learning difficulties have in spontaneously generalising their learning to different people and settings. One way to solve this is to teach in the natural environment in the first place — involving greater partnership with families and pushing aside the four walls of the school.

Although such aims need to be redefined and adapted to meet the needs of the children discussed in this book, the underlying principles are the same for all. Somehow, we have to ensure that children want to communicate, that there is someone to communicate with, that they have something to communicate about and that we teach them that communication is enjoyable and brings results. The success of non-vocal alternatives to speech owes much to these principles.

Clearly, children with severe communication problems do not learn this lesson as well as those described by Piaget and other psychologists. We can now map stages of cognitive and communicative development in terms of Piaget's six stages of sensori-motor development. We are also better able to describe what we mean by a functional communication curriculum. What we cannot do so well is to pinpoint the motivational and emotional needs of children who have less experience of successful and satisfying interactions with adults or other children. It is for this reason that the work reported here on assessment of emotional responses is so important. Similarly, the central concept of intentionality needs to be rethought in the light of the distinctive needs of the children who are the subject of this book.

The time has come to find a new balance between structure and stimulation. During the last decade, professionals have become much more proficient in the use of behavioural methods of teaching the individual. We now need to learn to make active and planned use of the environment to provide learning experiences and communicative demands which are directly related to the learning needs of the individual. This is not the same thing as merely teaching in the natural environment, nor is it a call for 'planned chaos'. It does call for a planned, systematic individualised instruction incorporating specific environmental elements.

Work such as that reported here springs from a vigorous and equal partnership between research and practice in which the needs of a particularly challenging group of people are clearly to the fore. Whether those needs can be better met in the future than in the past depends on the allocation of more time and resources both to professional training and to research. Since the prospects for this are far from encouraging, books like this have a particularly important contribution to make to the dissemination of ideas for better practice.

REFERENCES

Bower, T. (1974) *Development in infancy*, Freeman, New York

Cunningham, C. and Sloper, P. (1978) *Helping your Handicapped Baby*, Souvenir Press, London

Leeming, K., Swann, W., Coupe, J. and Mittler, P. (1979) 'Teaching language and communication to the mentally handicapped', *Schools*

Council Bulletin No. 8, Methuen/Evans Educational, London
McCartney, E. (1984) *Teaching mentally handicapped adults to communicate*, British Institute of Mental Handicap, Kidderminster
Mittler, P. and Preddy, D. (1981) 'Mentally handicapped pupils and school leavers: a survey in north west England'. In B. Cooper, (ed.) *Abilities and needs of mentally retarded children*, Academic Press, London

Introduction

Judith Coupe and Juliet Golbart

In April and September 1986 the British Institute for Mental Handicap (BIMH) organised one-day conferences on "Early Communication" in conjunction with Melland School, Manchester Local Education Authority and the Hester Adrian Research Centre, University of Manchester. These conferences, in Manchester and London, were attended by about 300 professionals and parents. In the following months the contributors to the conference received extensive feedback from the participants which led to the decision to disseminate our work in the form of this book, *Communication before Speech*. Inevitably, our thinking has progressed, so that the content of the book reflects the further development of our ideas and practice, rather than strictly those presented at the conferences. We are very grateful to the BIMH for providing a forum for the dissemination of our work, and indebted also to the many conference participants and colleagues whose contributions and feedback have pushed us on in new directions.

This book examines recent research on the acquisition of pre-speech communication skills by normally developing infants and demonstrates how this can be applied to children and adults with severe communication impairments. Many of these children and adults will be functioning within Piaget's sensorimotor stage of cognitive development (approximately birth to two years) and will include young children with language delay, infants and young children with moderate learning difficulties and children and adults with severe learning difficulties. The approaches described may also be of benefit to young children with physical handicaps or sensory impairments.

Starting with an explanation of contemporary research, the first chapter explores changes in theories of language acquisition and gives a detailed account of what the more recent theories tell us about the normal acquisition of communication skills from birth to 18 months.

Chapter 2 presents a structured approach which enables adults to interpret with sensitivity those early behaviours and expressions of emotion which convey an individual's likes, dislikes, wants and rejections at three levels of pre-intentional or 'affective' communication. Through this, adults can intervene and open up channels for furthering the communication process.

In Chapter 3, 'Assessment for Teaching Communication Skills, Kiernan describes the development and use of the Pre-Verbal Communication Schedule (PVCS) which represents a procedure for helping in programme formulation for non-verbal and minimally verbal children and adults. The chapter describes how the PVCS can be used to develop programmes which are pupil directed, rather than teacher or therapist directed.

Next, Chapter 4, 'Communication for a Purpose', examines why some previous approaches to teaching communication may have been unsuccessful. Using the principle that we learn to communicate in order to have some effect on the world around us, general strategies for promoting communication in the classroom, training centre or home are discussed.

Chapter 5 provides a method of teaching early meanings to children or adults who are beginning to act upon, understand and communicate about objects and events within their environment. Contexts and strategies for teaching within a meaningful routine are discussed along with a detailed account of how the approach can be generalised in the classroom or other everyday setting.

Finally, the last chapter considers an early communication curriculum and implications for practice. Part one of the chapter draws on the Curriculum Intervention Model and considerations for designing a curriculum are outlined. This reflects the 'how' whilst part two investigates the 'what' of teaching communication where the content of the previous chapters is drawn together and utilised to form a cohesive framework for selecting curriculum content. This chapter stresses the need to record while assessing and teaching.

Communication, however, does not occur only in teaching sessions, but as part of our everyday interactions. Hence, to understand how an individual communicates, typical communicative interchanges between that individual and those around them should be collected and analysed. We are currently developing strategies for recording, analysing and assessing which will be sufficiently sensitive to capture the interactions and early communications of students at these very early stages. Once these strategies have been finalised and found to be reliable, it will be easier to monitor progress in communication in natural settings.

This book contains no discussion of the relative merits of speech and sign or symbol systems. We feel strongly that we are working to develop *communication* through the easiest mode for individual learners and those with whom they want to communicate. Hence, spoken language, natural gesture, vocalisations, picture cards, photos, formal sign or symbol systems and written words are all both usable and appropriate. We know of no evidence to suggest that early communicators abandon speech in favour of 'easier' signs or symbols. The power of speech for communicating across distances and with unfamiliar people makes it more valuable than any other mode.

As editors, we feel that our multidisciplinary collaborative approach to tackling real issues in the contexts in which they occur is of great importance. The varied expertise of our contributors — teachers, speech therapists, psychologists and researchers — has provided a variety of perspectives on the teaching of communication while, at the same time, ensuring that our assessments and approaches to intervention have direct relevance and are practical for implementation in schools and training centres. Also, since parents are active contributors to the development of their child's communication skills, we have considered it essential to discuss and incorporate their views. Much of the 'research' in this volume has evolved through working parties involving a multidisciplinary group of professionals. With an emphasis on enhancing current approaches to meeting the educational needs of pupils, these teachers, nursery nurses, speech therapists, physiotherapists and psychologists have investigated many aspects of curriculum development. A group such as this certainly promotes and enhances exchange of ideas and information and provides a rich source and focus for feedback and dissemination. It also provides a forum for the establishment of collaborative research (Sinha, 1981).

1

Re-examining the Development of Early Communication

Juliet Goldbart

During the last ten to 15 years there has been an enormous expansion in research on how normally developing infants and young children acquire language. This research has culminated in new theories of language acquisition. We have found these theories exciting, even inspiring, in our attempts to devise intervention strategies for impaired communicators. Our own research has concerned mainly children and adults with severe learning difficulties. However, we are confident that our approaches are relevant to many other individuals at very early stages of language acquisition.

It could be argued that those of us working in more applied areas have been slow to respond to the implications of this new research. However, it seems likely that this stems more from the dominance of the prevailing theories of the 1960s and 70s than from any lack of interest in new work. Until the early 1970s, the study of language and language development was dominated by two main theories; Chomsky's Grammarian theory (Chomsky, 1957, 1965) and Skinner's Behaviourist theory (Skinner, 1957). These two approaches, which will be discussed in greater detail in Chapter 4, led to a very large number of intervention studies with children and adults with a wide range of types of language delay or disorder. Many of these studies concerned children and adults with severe learning difficulties, in particular those who were functioning at the one and two-word stage. As we will see later, these studies were not always very successful.

The scope of more recent research on normally developing infants and young children has been extremely broad and encompasses such areas as:

(1) The type of language input received by young children (Nelson, 1973; Snow, 1972).

(2) Early gestures and vocalisations (Bates, Camaioni and Volterra, 1975; Bruner, 1975).

(3) Different approaches to categorisation of first words and phrases (Benedict, 1979; Bloom and Lahey 1978).

(4) Differences among individuals in their routes to language learning (Lieven, 1978).

The findings of these studies can be unified, quite logically, into two new theoretical approaches. These theoretical approaches are usually described as the *psycholinguistic* approach — a semantic-cognitive theory — and the *sociolinguistic* approach — a sociocultural theory. These are, in fact, quite different approaches, but are by no means contradictory. In order to see how each has influenced the research and practice that we will be discussing in later chapters, it is important to consider their underlying principles.

THE PSYCHOLINGUISTIC APPROACH

This has three major underlying principles.

(1) The child's early utterances, which may preceed recognisable words, are expressions of semantic relationships, where semantics involves those aspects of language which are to do with the meaning and content of words or protowords (the forerunners of words). Thus, the first words or protowords that children produce express things to do with meaning and content. Bloom and Lahey (1978) propose the following as the first semantic relations expressed.

• Existence: The child comments on or acknowledges the existence of an object or entity, for example, 'What's that?' 'Shoe', 'This'.

• Nonexistence: The child comments on the absence of an expected object or entity, for example, 'Gone', 'Sock' with rising intonation.

• Disappearance: The child comments on or requests the disappearance of an object or entity, for example, 'All gone', 'Bye-bye'.

• Recurrence: The child comments on or requests that an

object, entity or event reappears, reoccurs or replaces one that has gone, for example, 'Again', 'More'.

(2) Semantic relations, these expressions of meanings and content, are an encoding of the child's existing knowledge about the world. So, when a child uses a word or a protoword they are, in fact, making some comment about something they understand about the world, some action or event in the environment. However, it must be remembered that the meanings do not exist out there in the world, they are imposed on events and object relations by the child (Palermo, 1982).

(3) Arising out of the first and second points, we can see that language development is built, at least in part, on cognitive development. That is, on the child's knowledge about objects and entities and the relationships between them.

The psycholinguistic theory can thus be seen to offer much in explanation of what we observe in the early utterances of young children. (For further details see Bloom, 1973; Greenfield and Smith, 1976). The approach also suggests certain intervention strategies, particularly the idea that the child needs experience of objects and events in their environment, and that this experience can be gained through interaction with people, with objects and, of course, through play. However, this theory does not explain why language and communication develop. Why should a child feel the need to express a cognitive relationship? Why should a child feel the need to tell you 'Ball gone'? For an explanation of this aspect, to find out why children learn to communicate, it is necessary to turn to the second theory.

THE SOCIOLINGUISTIC APPROACH

In the sociolinguistic approach, the sociocultural theory, the emphasis is on the child in a social setting. This approach has five fundamental principles.

(1) Language is acquired only if the child has reason to communicate. We see this as a crucial point, and it will underpin much of what is discussed later. The implication is that a child with language and/or learning difficulties or an adult with mental handicap is only going to learn to communicate if they have a reason, a purpose, for that communication. This reason could of course be social or material.

(2) As the child matures and produces more complex expressions, linguistic structure is initially acquired through decoding and understanding incoming linguistic stimulation. Hence, interactions between the language learner and more mature language users are likely to be very important.

Two further points follow on from (1) and (2):

(3) Language is learned in dynamic social interactions involving the child and mature language users. This emphasises the importance of positive contacts with adults, since it is they who provide the input to be decoded and understood.

(4) Language is first acquired as a more effective means of obtaining things that the child could previously get, or do, by simpler communication.

(5) Finally, children are active participants in the process of learning communication, and bring to this learning situation a set of behaviours, both social and cognitive, which allow them to benefit from the adults' facilitating behaviours. So, adults are playing their part in this dynamic interaction, but the language learner needs a set of social and cognitive skills if they are to benefit from adult facilitation.

Again, this theory has provided a number of clues which we have found particularly helpful in devising intervention strategies. The first is the importance of the child as an active participant in learning language and communication. The notion of the child as an active learner has prompted us to make use of Piaget's account of development in the sensori-motor period, the first two years of normal development (Piaget, 1952). Although we acknowledge the difficulties in establishing the precise relationship between cognition and language acquisition, we have taken the view that certain cognitive and perceptual prerequisites are necessary, but not sufficient, for the development of language and communication. As the language learner becomes older, however, it seems increasingly likely that a mismatch may arise between cognitive level and language level. This is a topic that requires much further investigation.

The second issue to emerge is the importance of giving the language learner real opportunities to communicate with mature language users; an issue which will be addressed in some detail later in the book.

It will be apparent that these two theories are not mutually exclusive; there is some overlap, and it is our view that they can be used in a complementary fashion. (For further discussion of both approaches see McLean and Snyder-McLean, 1978.) We recognise that there are risks inherent in applying research findings from normally developing children to children and adults with severe learning difficulties who may not follow normal developmental sequences (Greenwald and Leonard, 1979; Miller and Chapman, 1984). However, unless there is evidence to the contrary, the established developmental route seems the best to follow.

Let us now examine the stages in development according to the psycholinguistic approach. These will include aspects of cognitive, semantic and symbolic development. The ages are of course approximate and it cannot be assumed that having the cognitive behaviour necessarily implies that the semantic or symbolic behaviour will be established. The stages are drawn from Piaget's findings on the sensori-motor period (Piaget, 1952; Uzgiris and Hunt, 1975).

Table 1.1: Cognitive, semantic and symbolic development at stages 1 to 6 in Piaget's sensori-motor period

Stages	Approx. age (months)	Cognitive/semantic/symbolic development
1	0-1	(Reflex exercise) Selective looking
2	1-4	Early undifferentiated schemes: eg, mouthing, looking, holding
3	4-8	Intentionality established. Shaking, banging and other differentiated schemes, therefore cognitive roles being established
4	8-12	Cognitive roles expand. Appropriate use of familiar objects. In means-ends the goal is established prior to activity. Semantic roles start to be conveyed
5	12-18	Relational play then self-pretend play. First words, readily categorised by semantic role
6	18-24	Decentred-pretend play then sequenced pretend play. Complex series of gestures. Two-word utterances, syntactic developments

As can be seen from Table 1.1, at the very beginnings of development, the first month, there is only a limited amount that can really be described as cognitive development, certainly nothing that could be classed as semantic or symbolic development. Reflex exercise can be observed; if, for example, the tip of a finger is put in the groove of a baby's tongue sucking can be elicited as a reflex response. It is also suggested (Haith, 1980) that infants at this stage show selective looking, that is, babies have certain strategies which make their visual activity far more than random. Hence, if babies are awake and active, they will open their eyes; if they encounter darkness they will make a broad search of the environment; if they find light but no edges or contours they will again make a broad search. In areas of high contrast, a narrow search is made. Thus, it does seem that there is a little that we could describe as cognitive behaviour even at this very early stage.

Over the following three months infants engage in a range of undifferentiated schemes. These are actions on objects which are performed on a whole range of objects irrespective of what, to adults, the properties or functions of the objects are. Thus they can be seen as generalised and repeatable responses to things in the environment. Typically, these schemes include looking, mouthing and holding. During this stage, Piaget describes the infant as engaging in primary circular reactions. In these, if babies start a behaviour involving their own bodies which is found to be pleasurable, strategies exist to keep that behaviour going, but the goals are not set before the action sequence is begun and it is questionable whether the notion of a goal is at all appropriate at this stage.

During the third stage goals are still not set before starting action patterns. However, there is heightened interest in event outcome and it seems that goals are set once action sequences have started. Furthermore, these action patterns (or manifest-ations of cognitive roles) can now involve objects and events external to the baby. These are known as secondary circular reactions. This first establishment of a connection between means and ends is of paramount importance, since it is during this stage, at about the six months developmental level, that the infant acquires intentionality, the establishment of purposeful action on the environment.

Stage 4 sees these cognitive roles expanding. The infant now has greater experience with objects and a wider range of actions with objects. Familiar objects start to be used appropriately, the first one typically being drinking from a cup. In relation to the connection between means and ends, the child now establishes a goal prior to the start of an activity. The very beginnings of the communication of semantic roles can now be observed; having established a diversity of cognitive roles the child starts to communicate them to other people. Bloom and Lahey's (1978) account of the first semantic roles to be communicated has been given above (page 20). To communicate these semantic roles or early meanings at this stage the child uses looking, actions, gestures and/or vocalisations.

During stage 5, which lasts from around one year to 18 months, the child starts to engage in relational play. Children begin to relate objects together in play, putting spoons in cups, bricks in boxes and so on. In the second half of the stage, this develops into self-pretend play, feeding self with a spoon, pretend brushing own teeth. This is also the stage where children could be expected to produce their first words. Initially, these are likely to reflect the very early semantic categories described by Bloom and Lahey, but, during this stage, these categories expand to include a wide range of meanings which the child can now convey. Leonard (1984) has proposed the following list of semantic roles or notions as being those expressed at the single word and early two-word stage (see Table 1.2).

Stage 6 is really a transitional stage, a link into the pre-operational stage. In this stage, symbolic play develops, with the child showing decentred pretend play, for example feeding dolly

Table 1.2: Semantic notions

Semantic notion	What is being expressed
Nomination	Naming
Recurrence	Awareness of potential for reappearance or re-enactment
Denial	The rejection of a proposition
Non-existence	Recognition of the absence of an object that was present
Rejection	Prevention or cessation of an activity or appearance of an object
Action + object	An animate receives the force of an action
Location	Spatial relationship between two objects
Possession	An object is associated with someone or something
Attribution	Properties not inherently part of the class to which the object belongs
Experience + experiencer	Animate affected by event
Action + instrument	Inanimate causally affected in an activity

Source: Adapted from Leonard (1984; p. 144)

or daddy, brushing teddy's or mummy's hair. These actions then become sequenced, for instance feeding dolly, daddy and teddy or, a little later in the stage, undressing dolly, putting it in the bath, washing it, taking out of the bath and drying it and putting it to bed. These longer play sequences are echoed in the child's complex sequences of gestures, and then, towards the end of the stage, in two-word utterances and the beginnings of syntactic developments.

Our interest in this book is largely with what happens up to and including stage 5; communication development up to first words.

It is now necessary to turn our attention to development according to the other theoretical approach, the sociolinguistic approach. Here, our interest is in the way in which language learners come to acquire a functional use of language and communication (Figure 1.1).

From birth to about six months, caregivers accept a wide range of the baby's actions and vocalisations as meaningful. For example, when the caregiver is changing the baby's nappy the baby might blow a raspberry, to which the caregiver might say 'Does that feel better then?' or if the baby, having been taken out of her cot and put on the floor, kicks her legs the caregiver might say 'Yes, you like it down here don't you?' So the adult is imposing meaning on, or richly interpreting, the infant's actions or vocalisations. Interactions between the infant and caregiver at this stage usually take the form of periods of mutual gaze, baby and caregiver spending periods of time in eye contact and adult-directed turn-taking, where the adult talks to the baby and leaves spaces for the baby to fill, with sounds or actions. The baby's action is taken as a response and the 'dialogue' continues.

At around six months, as demonstrated in Figure 1.1, the baby is demonstrating some level of intentionality, the beginnings of intentional actions on the environment. Caregivers are reported as becoming much more selective (Gibb Harding, 1983). From this stage they interpret only certain actions or gestures as meaningful. Hence, by accepting only more and more clearly defined behaviours as communicative, we are shaping, building in for the infant, intentional communication, the concept that you can affect other people's behaviour by your own actions or vocalisations, that is, communication. Thus, a transition has taken place from purposeful action on the

Figure 1.1: Developments in the functional use of communication and language

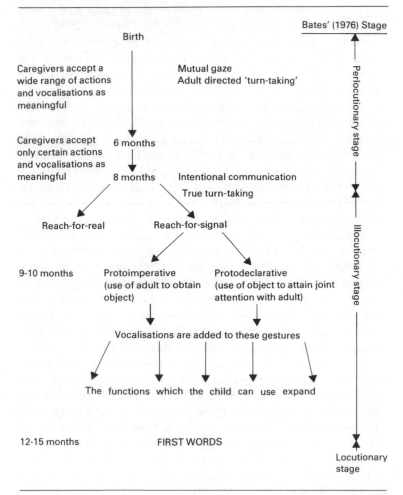

environment, that is intentionality, to intention to transmit some message, which would be intentional communication. At this stage the infant can engage in true turn-taking interactions with caregivers.

From this stage of intentional communication, the baby, who has for some time been reaching for things and picking them up, starts to use the reach for different purposes. The 'reach-for-real', reaching for something within reach in order to get hold of it, continues, but the baby also uses the 'reach-for-signal', reaching for something which is out of reach. By incorporating looking in the reach-for-signal, the baby communicates to the adult that he wants the thing he is reaching for (Bruner, 1975). This reach-for-signal then develops two clear functions: the proto-imperative and the protodeclarative (Bates, Camaioni and Volterra 1975). The first of these, the protoimperative, is really an extension of the reach-for-signal. It involves reaching for something and looking urgently from it to the person with whom you are trying to communicate. In the next stage this would also incorporate a vocalisation; for example the baby reaches for a banana in the middle of the table, looks from it to you repeatedly and says 'Uh! Uh! Uh!' The protoimperative can, therefore, be defined as using the adult to obtain an object.

The protodeclarative works in a rather different way. Here the intention is not to get an object, but to gain some kind of interaction or joint attention with the adult. In this case the reach gradually turns into a point, and, later in the stage, a vocalisation is added; for example, the baby points to the family cat and says 'Dah!' Hence, the protodeclarative can be defined as using an object to gain joint attention with the adult. Once this development has been achieved, babies are more active, directive partners in interactions, being able to direct adults' attention to things they want to communicate about.

In our experience, the use of protoimperatives and proto-declaratives starts at around nine or ten months with the gesture plus appropriate looking. Vocalisations start to be added shortly afterwards. Our observations suggest that the protoimperative and protodeclarative are used rather before Bates (1976) found (Bates suggests during sensori-motor stage 5). Bates reports that tool use is a pre-requisite for the use of these two functions; hence, Glenn's (1986) account of infants using infrared switching devices to operate a visual display from seven months developmental level adds some confirmatory evidence to our hypothesis. It may also suggest that, using new technology, behaviours analogous to tool use may be elicited before sensori-motor stage 5. In the following month or two, these two functions diversify further to enable the child to communicate a wide range of intentions or functions to people in their environment. These functions will be discussed in some detail in the third and fourth chapters of this book. From around twelve to 15 months, of course, these functions start to be communicated as words, though the use of gesture for communication does continue.

From 15 or 18 months, children and their caregivers engage in joint action routines (Snyder-McLean et al, 1984). These are frameworks for joint attention or joint action, formulated play routines engaged in first by adult and child or adult and children, but later by small groups of children on their own. In these routines the adult comments on the child's actions, thus mapping appropriate language onto what the child is doing. The sequences also provide an opportunity for the child to try out a wide range of communicative functions in a familiar and facilitative context. At this point it is clear that the findings of the two approaches have merged.

From this sociolinguistic, sociocultural approach, we have seen that the baby becomes an increasingly active and directive partner in communication, with progressively less of the burden of interpretation falling on the adult. The young child is showing increasingly sophisticated ways of communicating, from looking to gesture to gesture plus vocalisation to words (or signs or symbols), and, finally, it can be seen that the child is able to do increasingly varied things with this skill of communication.

The information gathered from the two more recent approaches to communication development can now be drawn together as an initial stage in planning a sequence for intervention. Some of the points can be implemented immediately in their own right, others will form the subject matter of later chapters.

First, and most obviously, it must be ensured that all learners are given a diversity of experiences to enable them to develop a range of schemes for acting on the environment. The transition from actions relating to self to actions relating to objects and people seems to be particularly problematic for individuals with profound and multiple handicaps. On the part of parents, teachers and other significant people in the language learner's environment, there is a need to develop sensitivity in order to recognise the point where the learner appears to have developed intentionality, and then to start shaping intentional communication. An assessment tool and intervention methods appropriate to this stage form the content of the following chapter. The establishment of intentional communication is, of course, just a beginning. It will become important to identify the best route for developing communication for each individual, so that maximum advantage can be taken of that person's existing skills. This will involve enhancing the strategies staff have for assessing and extending individuals' functional communication skills. Both these aspects will be considered in the third chapter.

In addition to working with individuals, it is necessary to consider how to foster the use of communication in everyday settings, at home, in training centres or workshops, at school and in the wider community. It cannot be assumed that skills taught in one setting will automatically generalise to other contexts. This needs to be planned for and involves a consideration of very general strategies for promoting communication which will be discussed in the fourth chapter. In moving towards the communication of semantic roles and the eventual use and understanding of single words, it is important to provide input to help learners encode their cognitive experiences. A detailed approach to teaching first meanings will be presented in Chapter five.

Finally, and perhaps most importantly, all these areas will need to be embedded in a curriculum which can be used readily in schools and training centres. This issue, and some ideas for subsequent planning stages will form the content of the final chapter of the book.

2

Affective Communication

Judith Coupe, Mark Barber and Debbie Murphy

When given a taste of salad cream Louise reacts. To an observer, most of her responses to the taste are centred around her face. Her mouth, and especially her tongue, become more active. Her tongue seems to push the salad cream forwards, lip activity increases, as does the movement of her eyes, and a slight frown appears. On a second presentation of the salad cream her lips close to prevent the spoon from entering her mouth. However, when Louise is given chocolate sauce she responds quite differently. Again her eye activity increases, as does the activity around her mouth, but in this instance her mouth movement is different. Rather than pushing the sauce away she appears to be spreading it around her mouth. In fact, on a second presentation she readily accepts the spoon full of chocolate sauce.

How do we know that Louise likes the chocolate sauce and dislikes the salad cream?

Our assessment suggests that she is functioning at a stage of pre-intentional communication and it is we who interpret her responses to stimuli and place meaning on them. When she is given salad cream to taste she reacts by frowning and increasing her tongue, lip and eye movements and we interpret this as conveying, "I don't like it". Louise is not intentionally communicating that she does not like it. She is purely reacting to salad cream itself. On the other hand, we can recognise from her behaviours that she likes the chocolate sauce. It is quite possible for us to interpret these responses and place accurate communicative meaning on them.

31

PRE-INTENTIONAL COMMUNICATION

For years, teachers, speech therapists and psychologists have struggled to understand and apply appropriate intervention strategies for pupils who function at a very early stage of communication. These pupils may be young infants with some form of communication delay, but a high proportion have severe learning difficulties which are often combined with sensory and physical handicaps. Results of a survey by Leeming et al (1979) indicate that just over a quarter (26.5 per cent) of pupils with severe learning difficulties are not yet imitating single words. Until recently there has been little in existence to sensitise teachers to the level of functioning of these pupils. Of course, detailed knowledge of the child is important and provides much information, but difficulties have arisen in utilising this information to plan subsequent teaching strategies.

As there is little available research on the early communicative development of children with severe learning difficulties, our theoretical background has necessarily incorporated findings of studies of normally developing infants. The works of Bates (1976), McLean and Snyder-McLean (1978), Snow (1972) and Thoman (1981) have been of significant value. It was felt important to examine social interaction prior to the establishment of intentional communication. Also, we were concerned with the relationship between this and cognitive development. Finally, we needed suggestions for intervention strategies which might be appropriate to classroom settings.

Thoman (1981) identified the notion of affective communication where the adult interprets and places meaning on the infant's responses to the environment. Bates' (1976) theory of pre-intentional communication is concerned with children who have not yet reached sensori-motor stage 4, particularly in the areas of means for obtaining a desired environmental event, object-related schemes and the development of visual pursuit and permanence of objects. (For further information on sensori-motor stages see Coupe and Levy (1985), Dunst (1980) and Uzgiris and Hunt (1975).) With children at this pre-intentional stage of communication Snow's (1972) work and that of McLean and Snyder-McLean (1985) highlight considerations for intervention.

These theoretical principles formed the foundation for the Affective Communication Assessment (ACA) by Coupe et al

(1985). Although speculative in concept, the ACA opens up channels for teaching and monitoring development — however slight.

THE AFFECTIVE COMMUNICATION ASSESSMENT

Given that the child exhibits a range of behaviours, for example facial expressions and body movements, it is likely that these will regularly occur in response to certain external stimuli. For the child who is functioning at a pre-intentional level, it is important for adults to be sensitive to these responses, to attach meaning to them and to respond as if they were a communicative signal. Thus a two-way process of communication can be facilitated which will incorporate some consistent responses to the child's feelings of like, dislike, want and reject. Through observations of the child's behaviours it is possible for the adult to identify those consistent repertoires of behaviours which express feelings and responses. This information can then be utilised to draw up and implement relevant and specific programmes of intervention.

To assess affective communication we are essentially concerned with placing communicative meaning on pupils' responses to a variety of internal and external stimuli. Sensitive interpretation is necessary and we have identified the four crucial meanings of like, dislike, want and reject. Of course many variations and extremes can be interpreted, as can other meanings such as distressed, hungry, tired, angry, puzzled and so on. Throughout this stage of pre-intentional communication a developmental sequence can be taken into account (see Chapter 6) which progresses through three levels:

Level 1: Reflexive. Social significance is assigned by adults to very early and reflexive behaviours produced in response to internal and external stimuli.

Level 2: Reactive. Social significance is assigned by adults to reactive behaviours, that is the way the child reacts to events and people within the environment.

Level 3: Proactive. The child's efforts to act on the environment become signals to the adult who then assigns communicative intent and meaning.

The ACA was developed as a tool for guiding adults to determine stimuli which might elicit strong positive and negative responses from children. Information gained will provide the basis for extending the child's repertoire of affective communication and lead towards intentional signalling. Indeed, through assessing the child in such detail it is possible to accumulate much information about the child's responses to a wide range of stimuli. These stimuli should take into account all sensory channels, that is auditory, visual, tactile, taste, smell as well as the environment itself. With knowledge of the setting conditions and systematic observation, the child's responses are readily interpreted as meanings and further observational checks can be made to determine the pattern, frequency and consistency of these behaviours. From this wealth of information the adult can make predictions regarding the child's repertoire of affective communication and plan appropriate programmes of intervention.

Stage 1: Observation

The adult first selects stimuli and situations to which the child is already known to respond. Using the Observation Recording Sheet (Figure 2.1), these stimuli are presented in turn and any responses by the child noted using either the categories of behaviour listed or others appropriate to the child. At the same time, the adult interprets the meaning thought to be conveyed by the child in response to each stimulus. These are usually: 'I want'/'I don't want' or 'I like'/'I don't like'. However, we have also received a neutral response.

During this initial stage as many observations of the child's responses to as wide a variety of stimuli as possible should be collected. It is important to ensure that the child is alert and comfortable and that optimum time of day, the context and so on are considered. A period of time must be allowed between the presentation of successive stimuli and for many children with severe learning difficulties and severe sensory impairment it is necessary to allow time for the stimulus to be registered in order subsequently to observe a response.

Stage 2: Identification

Having collated and interpreted numerous observations of the

Figure 2.1

ACA OBSERVATION Recording Sheet CHILD'S NAME:		STIMULI								DATE:						
HEAD	Turn — R/L. U/D															
	Activity ↑ ↓															
	Rotating															
	Other															
FACE	Frown															
	Smile															
	Anguish															
MOUTH	Activity ↑ ↓															
	Open/close															
	Tongue activity ↑ ↓															
	Contact															
EYES	Activity ↑ ↓															
	Open/close															
	Gaze															
	Localise/search															
HANDS	Activity ↑ ↓															
	Finger activity ↑ ↓															
	Contact															
ARMS	Reaching															
	Activity ↑ ↓															
LEGS	Activity ↑ ↓															
BODY	Activity ↑ ↓															
VOCALISATION	Utterance															
	Cry															
	Laugh															
	Other															
	AFFECTIVE COMMUNICATION Interpretation of child's behaviour															

Coupe, J., Barton, L., Barber, M., Collins, L., Levy, D., Murphy, D.

child's responses to a variety of stimuli, it is important to check for the consistency and quality of the behaviours by using the Identification Recording Sheet (Figure 2.2). From the stage 1 Observation Recording Sheet it is possible to identify the child's strongest responses of like, dislike, want and reject and gain further, more detailed information. The Identification Recording Sheet should be used by:

(1) Selecting the strongest responses.
(2) Listing those behaviours exhibited by the child.
(3) Re-presenting the stimuli and contexts to which the child exhibits strong responses.
(4) Recording the child's behaviours.
(5) Interpreting the child's responses.

Quite sensitive information can be gathered during this stage of identification and it is possible to note and establish any strong sequences of behaviours. It is also feasible to extend the range of stimuli by presenting others similar to those which are known to produce strong responses.

Stage 3: Intervention

At this stage, potentially communicative behaviours have been identified along with the stimuli and settings in which they are likely to occur. It therefore becomes easier to create optimum setting conditions through which the child can effectively communicate using a predicted repertoire of behaviours. The adult can then respond to the child in a relevant and consistent way throughout the day. Thus, the frequency of the child's communicative behaviours is likely to increase. It is essential for opportunities to be presented where the child is in a position to control or have an effect on the environment and the people within it. In this way, the child, however unintentionally, can initiate and respond to communication. By extending existing repertoires and capitalising on new behaviours we feel it is possible to generalise and shape the affective communication towards intentional signalling. It is important that intervention programmes lay stress on a two-way process of communication and that a warm, consistent social context is provided. The following seven aspects of interaction should be considered at all times with respect to both the adult and the child.

(1) Vocalisation: Respond to the child's vocalisations. Use the

Figure 2.2

ACA IDENTIFICATION	STIMULI										DATE:					
Recording Sheet																
CHILD'S NAME:																
AFFECTIVE COMMUNICATION																
Interpretation of child's behaviour																

Coupe, J., Barton, L., Barber, M., Collins, L., Levy, D., Murphy, D.

37

child's name using different vocal tones and modes such as whispering, calling or singing.

(2) Facial expression: React to and initiate smiling, laughing, frowning and so on.

(3) Body proximity: Generally it is important for the adult to be close to the child when interacting, particularly with their face near and clearly visible to the child.

(4) Eye contact/orientation of visual regard: If necessary the child's head or face can be moved to aid eye contact with the adult, or mutual regard of a relevant object.

(5) Physical contact: Touch the child's face or body. Prompt the child to touch the adult.

(6) Imitation: It is particularly important to imitate the child's own sounds or facial expressions.

(7) Turn taking: As much as possible, give the child time to respond to the adult. The adult can, in turn, respond to the child with an imitated or novel behaviour.

ACA: a study of Louise

Louise is a six-year-old child with severe learning difficulties and additional physical and visual handicaps. She is also on medication for epilepsy.

Vision

She is cortically blind, has nystagmus with a left divergent squint and an underdeveloped optic nerve. She responds to light stimulation but her functional vision is very limited.

Hearing

Louise has an acute sense of hearing. She responds positively to verbal and non-verbal sounds. Thus, hearing is a crucial sensory channel for her.

Physical competence

She has hypertonic cerebral palsy and is non-ambulant. Her movements are predominantly involuntary and reflexive in nature. Poor head control and a lack of trunk control inhibit functional position. Active, voluntary control is difficult to accomplish due to her primitive reflexes. Any voluntary movement is limited to head turning to her left (due to asymmetric tonic neck reflex her head turns to her right). This is important to consider as stimuli should be presented to her left. A check needs to be made to determine whether any localising response is reflexive or voluntary.

Communication skills

Louise is functioning at a stage of pre-intentional communication. She is an extremely sociable child and it is relatively easy for adults to interpret her likes and dislikes, wants and rejections. Louise uses strong repertoires of facial expressions, vocalisations and body movements. However, because of her sociability and pleasant disposition there is a danger that adults will over assume her level of functioning, that is her responses are often interpreted as signals.

Cognition

Louise's gross physical and visual limitations make it difficult to assess her level of cognitive functioning. Many of her behaviours are reflexive and link up to stages I and II in the sensorimotor period (see Uzgiris and Hunt, 1975). She has undifferentiated schemes and her basic behaviours incorporate grasping, mouthing, turn to light source and so on.

Discussions with Louise's teacher and nursery nurses enabled us to identify several situations where Louise had strong like or dislike, want or reject responses. By observing her in a structured way using Observation Sheet 1, we wished to obtain an indication of any current repertoires of behaviour which corresponded to these strong feelings. All stimuli were presented to her left side and we expected much of her observable behaviours to be centred around her head.

OBSERVATION

When given a taste of salad cream Louise reacted immediately by drawing her face into a wince (recorded as anguish on the left-hand side of the Observation Recording Sheet 1). Her mouth and especially her tongue were seen to become more active (recorded with a vertical arrow in the corresponding places). The tongue activity was apparently an attempt to push the cream forward in her mouth. Lip activity increased and an increase in the rate of eye movement was recorded, along with a slight arm bend. On second presentation of the salad cream, Louise's lips closed before the spoon passed between them. These behaviours were recorded as 'strong dislike' and 'refusal' respectively in the Affective Communication section of the sheet (see Figure 2.3).

On presentation of chocolate sauce, she behaved quite differently; again there was a noticeable increase in eye activity and lip and tongue movement, apparently attempting to position the sauce for swallowing. Her facial expression remained passive. Seen alongside the previous presentations of salad cream, Louise's recorded behaviours to the taste of chocolate sauce were quite similar, but the quality of reaction was very different and the chocolate sauce was obviously more welcome. Her response was interpreted to mean 'I like it'.

For a different stimulus, Louise was positioned on a soft floor mat whilst a member of staff banged her hands on the surface near her head. Louise immediately turned her head. Smiling, she slightly moved her arms, fingers and legs and produced an utterance. Her body also moved to the left. The initial increase in head activity was recorded as a surprise reflex, but subsequent recording showed that her head consistently moved to the left when she vocalised.

On presentation of the smell of her father's after shave, Louise opened her mouth, and an increase in eye activity was observed. Her facial expression remained passive and this was recorded as a gaze. When after three presentations she had shown the same behaviours it was felt that she had noticed the smell, but that her reaction to it was neutral.

Numerous other stimuli incorporating all senses were presented. These included a staff member sneezing which produced what was interpreted as a 'like' response, involving right-to-left movement of her head, a smile, increase in eye and mouth activity and a vocal utterance similar to that produced in the mat banging situation. On the recording sheet, after numerous stimuli had been presented, noticeable similarities began to appear particularly in behaviours involving strong likes and dislikes. In her repertoire of behaviours which showed likes and wants, utterances and head rotations occurred along with smiles and increased eye activity. Her repertoires of behaviours which showed dislikes or rejections, involved slight arm and leg

Figure 2.3

HEAD group	Observation	CHOCOLATE SAUCE	TARTARE SAUCE	'SPACE DUST'	'SNEEZE'	SLAPPING SURFACES CLOSE BY	HERB + SPICE SALTS	WHISPER	DRINK OF WATER	SALAD CREAM	GARLIC GRANULES	MUSTARD	'NAME'	HONEY	PEANUT BUTTER	LEMONADE	FATHER'S AFTERSHAVE	TICKLE
ACA OBSERVATION Recording Sheet — CHILD'S NAME: LOUISE									DATE:									
HEAD	Turn – R/L. U/D	L→R	L	R→L	L	L→R	L		L→R	L→DR	L→R	L→R	L	U		F	L→R	R→L
HEAD	Activity ↑↓			↑		↑ SUR-PRISE	↓		↑		↑	↑	↑	↑	↑			↑
HEAD	Rotating						✓						✓					
HEAD	Other			✓		✓						BACK ✓						
FACE	Frown							✓										
FACE	Smile		✓	✓	✓	✓		✓					✓	✓		✓		✓
FACE	Anguish						✓			✓		✓						
MOUTH	Activity ↑↓	↑	↑	↑	↑		↑			↑	↑	↑		↑	↑	↑	↑	↑
MOUTH	Open/close	O	C			O	C	O	C	C	C	C	O	O		O	O	O
MOUTH	Tongue activity ↑↓	↑	↑	↑			↑			↑	↑	↑		↑	↑	↑	↑	↑
MOUTH	Contact															✓		
EYES	Activity ↑↓	↑	↑	↑	↑	↑		↑	↑	↑	↑	↑	↑	↑	↑	↑	↑	↑
EYES	Open/close			O/C														
EYES	Gaze			✓												✓	✓	
EYES	Localise/search	✓		✓		✓		✓	?	✓			✓		✓			✓
HANDS	Activity ↑↓					↑			↑				↑	↑				
HANDS	Finger activity ↑↓					↑										↑		
HANDS	Contact																	
ARMS	Reaching																	✓
ARMS	Activity ↑↓	↑	↑	↑		↑	↑		↑	↑		↑			↑	↑		↑
LEGS	Activity ↑↓		↑			↑	↑			↑	↑							↑
BODY	Activity ↑↓				↑L													↑
VOCALISATION	Utterance			✓	✓	✓		✓					✓					✓
VOCALISATION	Cry																	
VOCALISATION	Laugh					✓										✓		
VOCALISATION	Other	✓																✓
AFFECTIVE COMMUNICATION Interpretation of child's behaviour		LIKE	DISLIKE	AWARE	STRONG LIKE	STRONG LIKE	MILD DISLIKE	LIKE	REJECT	STRONG DISLIKE	DISLIKE	DISLIKE	LIKE	WANT	LIKE	LIKE	NEUTRAL	STRONG LIKE

Coupe, J., Barton, L., Barber, M., Collins, L., Levy, D., Murphy, D.

flexions, lip closures and appropriate facial expressions of 'frown' and 'anguish'.

IDENTIFICATION

Those repertoires of behaviours which were interpreted to convey strong likes and dislikes, wants and rejections were checked for consistency. Louise's repertoires of behaviour were listed down the left-hand side of the Identification Recording Sheet (see Figure 2.4). The stimuli which had provoked these reactions, along with other similar stimuli suggested by classroom staff, appeared at the top of the list. The anticipated responses were observed. Furthermore, a consensus of agreement was reached by several observers. As with the initial observations, care was taken with the order of presentations so as to avoid the satiation of one sense (such as taste). Also, periods of settling-down time were given especially after strong reactions to presented stimuli. In this way responses would not intrude on each other. Louise was found to vocalise strongly in situations involving movement when swung from side to side by a staff member, and in the mat-slapping situation vocal utterances were consistently given. These situations appeared to give her strongest 'like' responses. Her most emphatic 'reject' responses occurred in situations where certain smells and tastes were presented to her. Reactions centred around her mouth and arm movements. From the wealth of information gained about Louise's likes and dislikes, wants and rejections it was possible to determine a strategy of intervention.

INTERVENTION

Once the identification of Louise's repertoire of behaviours had been checked for consistency, strategies of intervention were designed. At present social significance could be assigned to the way she reacts to events and people within her environment, also Louise's efforts to act on her environment have become signals to adults who can then assign communicative intent. However, as yet she shows no evidence of signalling communicative intentions to others. The information collated enabled us to capitalise on her efforts to act on people and events within

Figure 2.4

ACA IDENTIFICATION — Recording Sheet — STIMULI — DATE:

CHILD'S NAME: LOUISE

	SLAP MAT CLOSE TO HER	WATER	NAME	SALAO LAGAM	SWING	HONEY	WHISPER NAME	VIGOROUS TICKLE	ROCKING	LIFT ABOVE HEAD	MILK DRINK	GARLIC GRANULES	FATHER'S OR DAD'S AFTERSHAVE	SQUEAKY TOY	TOUCH IN EYE	SNEEZE	MUSTARD
HEAD TURN 4R/U/D	R→L	L→R		L→R		R→L		RO-TATE		RO-TATE	L	L→R		R→L		R→L	L→R
HEAD ACTIVITY ↑↓	↑	↑	↑	↑	↑	↑	↑	↑	↓			↑	↑		↑	↑	↑	✓
FROWN		✓		✓								✓					✓
SMILE			✓			✓			✓					✓	✓		
MOUTH ACTIVITY	↑		↑	↑		↑		↑	↓	↑	↑	↑	↑	↑			↑	↑
MOUTH OPEN/CLOSE	O	C		C	O	O	O	O		O	O	C	O			O	C
TONGUE ACTIVITY ↑↓	↑			↑		↑		↑	↓	↑	↑	↑	↑			↑	↑
EYE ACTIVITY ↑↓	↑	↑	↑	↑	↑	↑	↑	↑	↓	↑	↑	↑	↓	↑	↑	↑	
LOCALISATION SEARCH		✓			✓	?						✓		✓	✓	✓	
HAND ACTIVITY ↑↓	↑			↑		↑	↑					↑		↑			↑
ARM ACTIVITY ↑↓	↑	↑		↑	↑		↑										
UTTERANCE	↑	✓		✓		✓	✓							✓	✓		
LAUGH	✓			✓		✓	✓									✓	
LEG ACTIVITY	↑	↑		↑								↑					↑
AFFECTIVE COMMUNICATION — Interpretation of child's behaviour	STRONG LIKE	REJECT	LIKE	STRONG REJECT	STRONG LIKE	WANT	LIKE MED.→STRONG	STRONG LIKE	LIKE	STRONG LIKE	WANT	REJECT	NEUTRAL	LIKE	NEUTRAL	LIKE	STRONG REJECT

Coupe, J., Barton, L., Barber, M., Collins, L., Levy, D., Murphy, D.

her environment and shape those signals towards a stronger, more intentional two-way process of communication. The seven aspects of interaction were considered.

Vocalisation

Louise was found to 'like' and enjoy strong physical contact and movement. In these contexts we know that she will vocalise and smile consistently. It was felt important that a strategy should be identified to develop her vocalisation into a 'want' signal. For instance, an adult should hold Louise in her arms and swing her from side to side, then stop. Louise could be predicted to vocalise in response to this which would be interpreted as 'like'. However, in order to shape this vocalisation towards a communicative signal for 'want' the adult should wait for Louise to vocalise, at which point she will receive a further swing. This same sequence could be generalised to a variety of situations thus, vocalisation would be given a consistent and highly rewarding consequence.

Facial expression

Louise's facial expression is her most effective channel of affective communication, giving as it does a consistent indicator of her likes and dislikes, wants and rejections, particularly in relation to tastes and smells. As previously discussed, on a second presentation of salad cream and other undesirable tastes, Louise pursed her lips so that a further presentation was impossible. This was felt to be a strong 'reject' reaction. Our intervention strategy would be that after being given an initial taste of, for instance, salad cream it would be offered a second time in which case Louise would be in a position to communicate 'reject' as a refusal. As a result, staff would consistently acknowledge the signal and hence, Louise would have more control over her environment.

Body proximity

Louise cannot control the distance between herself and others.

It is important, therefore, to design a pattern of body positioning which allows adults to see and feel her reactions to stimuli. In this way an optimum setting for interaction can be created.

Eye contact

Prior to completing this assessment Louise's vision was considered to be too limited to be considered as a priority for intervention. However, her responses indicate that she has a level of competence which enables her to respond to light sources, moving shapes and, of course, the presence of people. Perhaps, as yet, this cannot be considered a priority channel for intervention, but close observation of her responses to visual stimuli should be monitored.

Physical contact

Although physical contact is difficult for Louise to initiate, it was felt to be most important. Louise is very aware of the presence of an adult. Indeed, because of her strong responses to physical contact and being cuddled, this was felt to be an important priority in drawing and responding to her 'like' and 'want' responses.

Imitation

Louise vocalises and produces cooing sounds. Whenever possible staff will imitate these vocalisations, giving time for her to respond. This relates very closely to the final aspect of intervention — turn taking.

Turn taking

Through vocal play or more physical activity Louise can be taught to establish a more controlled sequence of turn taking. Whilst being pulled to a sitting position by her hands Louise shows an increase in shoulder movements. This can be established as a turn-taking play routine where, after a few sequences

45

of being pulled into a sitting position and lowered down again, the adult can pause to allow Louise to move her shoulders as her turn in the routine. Similarly, a play routine can be established when Louise is lying down where the adult bangs on the mat near to her head. Louise will be predicted to vocalise and laugh in this situation and these behaviours can be utilised as Louise's turn.

A PARENT'S PERSPECTIVE

Louise's mother felt that for the first time they have a summary of her abilities in writing 'I feel as if we have known this all along but the Affective Communication Assessment has brought it to the forefront. It will help to explain her level to family and friends. It is true that a lot of people expect too much of her, now we can explain about interpreting her behaviour'. Louise's father works away during the week and he has seen the progress which, although slight, is noticeable. To capture her on video and have the assessment documented is important. 'She has come on more this year than any other year. As far as I can see this assessment must have helped to sensitise all the staff who work with her to get the best out of her. She responds so much more. I have always been able to get a smile out of Louise but now she can shout. She joins in with people around her and it matters, it helps with friends and family because now we know how to get a response from Louise and how to interpret it. We can tell them what to do with her to get a good response. Before, friends always used to pick her up and talk to her but they did not get the response which they are getting now'.

Louise has a wide range of likes and wants but few dislikes. As these are mainly to do with food her mother felt that it was difficult to always respond to the dislikes and rejects because she must eat. However, where she can she gives Louise a choice. 'For instance we know that Louise doesn't like water so we might give her this and if she doesn't want it, will give her a cup of tea instead.' The seven considerations for intervention have helped her greatly. 'I can now incorporate imitation with turn taking, using her own vocalisations. When she shouts, I shout and vice versa. We are using eye contact, physical contact, body proximity and facial expression. Bedtime is good for this as it is the one time of day when we are alone together. This is a lovely time where I spend ages using all aspects of communication.'

In planning where to go next Louise's mother felt confident: 'Now if I am not in the room with Louise she shouts, whereas before she would just lie or sit and be quite happy where I put her. She is initiating much more and not just responding. I think she is definitely trying to join in, for instance if I talk to her sister Emily, Louise will join in the conversation. I know that she is not intentionally communicating anything yet. It is still a matter of other people having to interpret everything for her. With her being so disabled her main form of signal can only be vocal or facial expression. We want more of this and can now see how it can be developed.'

The Affective Communication Assessment had been presented at a recent parents' meeting. Louise's mother felt that all the parents of profoundly handicapped children who were at the meeting wanted the assessment to be used with their children. She thought seeing the video enabled parents to understand and see the value of affective communication. In fact, whatever the child's level of development she felt it would be helpful for parents if video was used during assessments. In this way parents and staff could see how each child had improved. Indeed, for Louise: 'It seems to just all slot together now. Just like a jigsaw puzzle and we have captured it all on video.'

3

Assessment for Teaching Communication Skills

Chris Kiernan

Two groups of pupils in schools for children and young people with severe learning difficulties present a greater-than-usual challenge to teachers and other professionals responsible for their education and developmen'. Pupils with sensory and physical impairments may deviate substantially from 'normal developmental sequences' because of these impairments, show-ing highly individual patterns of acquisition of skills and a failure to develop speech. A second group are those pupils who, although their physical development may be normal and their vision and hearing apparently adequate, do not develop speech. Both groups may show problem behaviours but it is the latter group who typically display problems which may be related to inability to communicate even basic needs through speech.

The significance of these groups has increased as the educa-tion of pupils with severe learning difficulties has evolved. Methods of education which have been successful with other pupils are often predicated on the ability to follow verbal instruction and to model such verbal input in the acquisition of speech, or to respond to speech input as part of an activity-based curriculum. Multiply impaired and non-verbal pupils have difficulty in responding to such methods. Behaviour modification techniques have had greater success, almost certainly because they rely less on the understanding of speech. However, serious questions can be raised about the appro-priateness of behavioural approaches for teaching in this area (Kiernan, 1984).

In order to appreciate these problems, we need to look at the historical development of work on the acquisition of speech. Early studies of normal development tended to concentrate on the acquisition of vocabulary. This rather arid approach was replaced by the work of Chomsky (1957, 1965) who focused attention on the acquisition of syntactic rules as a basis for language. Chomsky's approach suggests strongly that knowledge of syntactic rules is inbuilt and unfolds as the normal child interacts with adult language. He suggested that we need to assume some measure of 'pre-wiring' if we are to account for the speed with which language is acquired and the similarities of acquisition across cultures.

Chomsky argued that acquisition of syntax is the key to language development. Slobin and others (e.g. Slobin, 1971) argued that the acquisition of semantics and meanings, through cognitive development was prior to the acquisition of syntax. The child acquires syntax to express meaningful relationships which he or she has encoded. Both approaches relegate the role of social interaction and teaching, to a secondary position in the development of language. Within the Chomsky framework the social environment supports acquisition through providing models. The semantic model gives it a slightly more active role. Here adults can facilitate development by ensuring that the child is exposed to environments through which cognitive development may occur and by providing and prompting language models which will allow the child to encode experience.

In the mid-1970s Bruner and others developed an alternative approach which has yet to be adequately assimilated in teaching pupils with severe learning difficulties. This approach draws the distinction between language as a system through which the individual encodes reality and communication, the ability of the individual to affect his or her social environment through the use of speech and non-verbal communication. There are several critical differences between language and communication so defined. The normal child is able to communicate in the sense of affecting people in his or her environment by the age of six months, well before language in the sense of inner representation of reality emerges. At this stage, and throughout life, communication may involve a range of non-verbal means, such as pushing and pulling, eye pointing, looking, or emotional expression. Speech is not a prerequisite to communication although obviously speech is the prime mode of communication in normal society. The approach also argues that the motive for acquisition of speech is that it allows the child to interact socially, to control the acquisition of goods and services and attention. Indeed, the ultimate proposition is that syntax is acquired because it helps the child to express increasingly complex modes of interaction.

This approach gives parents, teachers and other professionals a radically different role in teaching. If communication skills are to be developed the teacher needs to identify and foster needs and interests, and to facilitate social responsiveness so as to ensure that the pupil wants to interact with other people. A rounded approach to language teaching would see much of this interaction within the context of a cognitively based approach, in which the pupil is motivated to express evolving cognitive structures in interaction, and the mapping of syntactic skills on increasingly complex cognitive structures. Bruner (1974-5) argued that there were two fundamental types of interaction, those involving the child controlling adults in order to satisfy needs and deliver services, and those of a more directly social nature in which the child controls adult attention for its own sake (see also Bates, Camaioni and Volterra, 1975; and Chapter 1). These two broad groups of communicative act can be subdivided in a variety of ways (Atkinson, 1982). The child learns how to request but also how to say no, to protest and to hold adult attention through various strategies. For example, the child may hold attention by responding to requests by complying, as in naming tasks. Or the child may hold attention by calling attention to interesting objects or events, to things which he or she has done which he feels will achieve adult attention, either positive or negative, or, at a more advanced level, by reporting interesting events.

This type of analysis has an important feature. Different communicative acts can be realised through varying levels of cognitive and syntactic sophistication. A request for a toy may be realised through the child pointing repeatedly to the toy and vocalising loudly. The same act may be encoded as 'car', 'give car', 'give me car', 'give me car *now*', 'stop what you are doing and give me that car immediately', or a whole variety of syntactic structures of differing form and complexity. Similarly increasing cognitive sophistication, along with syntactic sophistication, may be reflected. The act may be expressed as 'give me the green car with white stripes which is next to the red posting box'.

The central point is that analyses in terms of communicative acts cut across syntactic and semantic skills. These analyses represent a different way of viewing speech and other means of communication. But, just as with syntactic and semantic skills, the child needs to learn different types of communicative act.

TEACHING OF LANGUAGE AND COMMUNICATION SKILLS

The teaching of language and communication skills to pupils with severe learning difficulties reflects theoretical developments rather poorly. Although this divide between practice and theory is common it seems to be particularly undesirable in this field, if for no other reason than that the needs of pupils are substantial and their progress is typically very slow; they need all the help that they can get. This section will characterise teaching in a very broad way. Inevitably, this characterisation will do poor justice to the efforts of some schools, but what is intended is to give a broad and, hopefully, fair summary of what seems to happen in the majority of schools.

In general teaching appears to stress acquisition of comprehension rather than expressive skills. At a basic level strategies derived from behaviour modification involve tasks in which the pupil is taught to follow simple signed or spoken instructions: 'come here', 'sit down', 'hands down', usually with a simple spoken or material reward. Or the pupil may be taught simple discriminations: 'show me the cup', 'give me the doll', again with verbal or material reward. At a more complex level this type of comprehension training may be geared to some concept of cognitive training or symbolic play. The Derbyshire Language Scheme (Knowles and Masidlover, 1982) relies heavily on the teaching of comprehension skills within a curriculum which reflects a mixture of semantic and syntactic concepts (Kiernan, Reid and Goldbart, 1987).

These tasks reflect two broad objectives. On the one hand, simple instruction following may be seen as primarily a way in which behavioural control is established. Receptive vocabulary training and the teaching of more complex comprehension skills reflect the idea that comprehension precedes expression in the acquisition of speech. This notion, although broadly supported by empirical research, ignores the fact that the two types of skills are essentially independent. Listener skills and speaker skills obviously involve different elements and need different forms of teaching. The teaching of expressive skills takes a

51

variety of forms. The non-verbal or minimally verbal pupil may be taught to imitate actions or sounds. The teacher may say 'look Andrew, do this' (raise hands). Andrew matches the model and the teacher rewards him with a generalised 'good boy, Andrew'. The overall objective here may be to develop generalised imitative skills which can then be used in a range of learning situations. How often this objective is realised is not clear.

Imitation training is often employed in building basic vocabulary. The pupil may be shown pictures or objects in a teaching session and asked to name them: 'look Sue, what's this?', 'brush', 'yes, it's a brush'. This strategy is commonly used in the teaching of manual signs where the Makaton approach (Walker, 1978) advocates teaching naming as a foundation stage. The assumptions underlying much of this teaching are that it is developmentally relevant; it is argued that naming is the first level of development of a normal child, and that, once the pupil has the vocabulary, he or she will be able to use it when he wants. Both of these assumptions can be questioned. Developmental studies suggest that, although naming may be an early function, the socially relevant requesting of goods and services may be more critical in acquisition. In addition, the possession of a word does not necessarily mean that it will be used. Naming in response to the teacher's question is a specific type of communicative act. If, as seems likely, an important aspect of learning to communicate is the acquisition of a range of different communicative acts, requesting, negating and so on, teaching the child one type of act will not necessarily lead him to learn others. Indeed, teachers commonly complain that pupils, especially pupils being taught signs, 'know the signs but don't use them spontaneously'. In other words they can and do respond readily in a naming task but do not generalise to using the vocabulary in other communicative contexts. In practice, the pupil may not know how to perform communicative acts or, if he or she does, may not have learned that signs or words can be used as a medium for communication except in response to requests for naming.

Other teaching strategies are more clearly derived from theoretical propositions. Some are directed at teaching syntax. A pupil may be shown a variety of pictures which are exemplars of particular syntactic structures, 'John has a brick', 'John has two bricks' or 'Mummy's old cooker', 'Tom's broken bike',

'Jill's dirty teddy'. At the teaching level these tasks tend to be restricted to the communicative act of describing, again in response to the teacher's questions. Any generalised use of syntactic structures, for example in the pupil reporting what has happened on the way to school or at home, is to be developed by the teacher as an independent part of the curriculum and may be omitted if the teacher believes that generalisation will occur 'spontaneously'. Even when teachers employ report sessions these are often highly structured and do not encourage deviation from a set format.

In general the strategies described so far can be characterised in two ways. First of all, as we have seen, they tend to teach a very restricted set of communicative acts, naming or describing. The pupil is expected to generalise content to other communicative acts but these are not necessarily taught. Secondly the strategies are very much teacher directed. Indeed it is often hard to see where 'communication' can come in. The teacher knows the answer to the question before he or she asks it, and the pupil will very often be aware of this. In this context these strategies may simply teach the pupil that signing or saying words is just yet another trick which teachers require of you in school. The power of signs and words to influence what other people do may completely escape the pupil. This likelihood is particularly strong with less able pupils.

Some strategies break through this essentially restricted teacher-directed format. The role-reversal strategy used within the Derbyshire Language Scheme involves a shift in control of situations from teacher direction to pupil direction once the pupil has learned relevant structures. In a real way this 'transfer of power' should help pupils to learn how to use speech or signing in a communicative way, to say what *they* want to say rather than to respond to teacher requests. However, the role-reversal strategy is easier to use with more able students, and less able students appear to be commonly viewed by teachers as only responsive to the more directive techniques involved in teaching comprehension and naming tasks.

THE DEVELOPMENT OF THE PRE-VERBAL COMMUNICATION SCHEDULE

The purpose of the Pre-verbal Communication Schedule (PVCS)

53

(Kiernan and Reid, 1987a,b) is to allow teachers and other people working with pupils with minimal verbal or signing skills to identify the pupil's current abilities and to develop teaching programmes. The central argument is derived from the theoretical outline presented earlier. It suggests that, in order to learn communicative skills, in part as a foundation for language development, teaching should allow the pupil to control his or her environment, to allow him to make choices, to express preferences, to negate and to benefit pleasurably from interaction. In other words, rather than being teacher directed teaching should be pupil directed.

The approach has several consequences. As we will see, the PVCS directs attention at the quality of the pupil's interaction with other people. If the pupils are to want to communicate it seems reasonable that they should want to interact with others. In addition, if he or she is to communicate, the pupil must have something to communicate about, some needs or interests. The pupils' existing communication system will give an indication of the range and type of communicative act which they can already perform. And for those pupils with sensory or physical impairment it is clearly important that we know what these impairments are before we develop programmes using words, signs or graphic symbols.

The PVCS was developed initially because we were trying to evolve programmes for non-verbal and minimally verbal children. A trawl of existing assessment procedures showed that the majority asked few questions about the abilities of such children and paid no attention to the way in which children used their skills in affecting their environment. So an item might read 'uses single words', or 'uses two words together' or 'uses prepositions' without asking how these skills were used. In addition there were no procedures available to guide teachers in selecting alternative or augmentative communication systems, sign languages or symbol systems. The first stage in development of the schedule was to gather any items from other assessment procedures which appeared to be relevant. These were modified to exclude composite items, for instance 'shows motor and vocal imitation skills', and amplified to make the mode of communication more clear. For example, requesting was broken down into requesting by pushing or pulling, pointing, looking, vocalising and so on. Other items were devised to cover gaps indicated by our knowledge of the communicative and other skills of pupils and by the theoretical and empirical literature.

Once a reasonably coherent set of items had been constructed we asked a group of experienced teachers to try out the PVCS with one or more of their non-verbal or minimally verbal pupils. They were then interviewed in detail in order to identify ambiguous items or items which were composite items for their pupils. They were also asked to point out any communicative behaviours that their pupils showed which were not covered by the PVCS. A revised version of the schedule was then scored independently by pairs of teachers for 48 pupils, all classified as severely mentally handicapped. These data formed the basis for a study of inter-rater reliability. The protocols of 90 pupils were used in a study of the factorial structure of the PVCS and of analyses in terms of communicative acts. An independent study, involving 30 respondents, provided a basis for further assessment of the validity of the PVCS. We will discuss the reasons for these studies, and their outcome, in the course of the following sections.

THE STRUCTURE OF THE PVCS

The PVCS comprises the schedule itself and a manual which describes the scoring methods and the interpretation of the information gathered. The schedule consists of 195 items. The majority are checklist items in which the respondent notes whether the ability or behaviour is one which is shown by or characteristic of the pupil. A few items, mostly concerned with motor imitation and the understanding of non-vocal communication, ask the respondent to test the pupil on simple tasks. We opted for a checklist and test approach rather than an observational approach for several reasons. We were interested in behaviours which may be fairly rare or only occur under particular circumstances. It was clear that teachers and other people interacting constantly with pupils would be in a position to remember relevant behaviours when prompted. To this degree the PVCS represents a method of eliciting and organising existing knowledge. We suggest that the PVCS is completed in consultation with other people, including parents, who know the pupil well. Furthermore, checklists can be completed outside direct teaching time. Observation, on the other hand, is time consuming and can interfere with other activities.

The items in the PVCS are grouped into 27 sections and the sections themselves fall into five clusters. These cover pre-communicative behaviour, skills and abilities which seem relevant to the evolution of various modes of communication; imitation; informal communicative behaviour; understanding; and existing use of formal means of communication, that is words, signs or symbols.

Pre-communicative behaviour

Since we were interested in the full range of communicative modes we included several sections to cover the pre-requisites of signing and symbol use. These assess the pupil's vision and ability to direct gaze, the use of visual cues through, for example, the ability to recognise people directly or through photographs and to match objects or pictures. All can be indicators of likely facility in learning to use pictures or symbols as a means of communicating. Assessment of the pupils' skill in controlling their hands and arms and in simple motor imitation is more directly relevant to the decision as to whether to use signs or symbols as a means of communication. Clearly, if pupils have very limited control of their hands and/or poor imitative skills, the use of signing as an expressive mode would be questionable.

The potential for reliance on speech as a mode of communication is assessed through the pupil's hearing and listening skills, coverage of their existing repertoire of sounds, ability to control speech musculature (breathing, eating and voluntary breath control) and the consistency in use of noise in play. Vocal imitation is also examined. In these assessments, and others, the PVCS does not pretend to provide exhaustive analysis. It is assumed that information from specialist procedures will also be sought, especially if the PVCS suggests that the pupil has substantial problems with hearing or muscular control.

In the introduction to this chapter we stressed the vital role of motivation in communication. Pupils should have something about which they want to communicate but, ideally, should also find interaction sufficiently pleasurable to want to communicate as a means of interaction. This thread is picked up in sections concerned with needs, interests and preferences, the non-communicative expression of emotion and social interaction.

These latter sections assess the degree to which the pupil is socially and emotionally withdrawn or outgoing. If the pupil is socially outgoing and emotionally expressive then we can be clearer in the assessment of needs, interests and preferences and, potentially, build on these traits in establishing positive interaction and communicative expression of interests, likes and dislikes. Withdrawn pupils would need a component of their programme designed to break through social avoidance, and greater emphasis on establishing the notion of expression of choice.

The PVCS includes a section assessing the pupil's ability to sing and respond to music. There are a few informally reported case studies of children who have been unable to speak but able to articulate words within songs. One approach which has been claimed as successful with these pupils has been to teach them to sing requests and other verbal communications, with the sung element being gradually faded as the pupil assumes normal speech. The mechanism underlying this treatment is a matter for speculation.

Imitation

The PVCS includes assessment of motor and vocal imitation for two reasons. Imitative skills index levels of attention to other people and the ability to conceptualise the other person's behaviour which are useful in understanding how well the pupil responds to others. They also reflect the pupil's level of skill in matching the behaviour of the other person. This can be important in the assessment of potential for learning signs and words. Furthermore verbal and motor modelling are important teaching strategies in learning speech or sign language. Indeed, if the pupil shows poor imitative skills, we would suggest that a component of imitation training should be included as part of any programme. However, this does not need to be an entirely static, teacher-led activity. Imitation training can be built in to programmes in which the pupil is learning to express preferences in asking for goods and services (Kiernan and Jones, 1985).

Informal communicative behaviour

Nine sections of the PVCS are devoted to assessing the pupil's existing informal repertoire of communicative behaviour. The sections cover communication through whole body action (for example, stiffening to resist being dressed), through eye pointing, pointing with hands or arms, giving, manipulation, pushing and pulling other people, and gestures. Several of these sections relate directly to potential for the use of sign language in the absence of vocal skills. The communicative use of sounds, judged in relation to scores on the relevant pre-communicative sections, and vocal imitative ability, can give clues on potential for speech.

In general we would urge that all programmes should include a component directed at developing speech or vocal expression. The evidence for many case studies suggests that non-verbal pupils in sign language programmes can develop speech (Kiernan, 1983; Kiernan, Reid and Jones, 1982). There are many ways in which this could come about but it is very difficult to predict what is going to happen in an individual case (Kiernan, Reid and Goldbart, 1987). It is therefore worth including a speech training component in a programme even if the pupil's potential for speech appears initially to be very limited. The pupil's use of pictures and objects as a means of communication is also covered. Great facility here, coupled with poor vocal skills and, for example, poor physical functioning and motor imitation skills, would suggest that pictures or symbols be tried as a means of expressive communication.

This cluster of sections also assesses the pupil's communicative expression of emotion, for example crying to get attention, and his or her skills in manipulating the emotions of other people. We have worked with pupils who will 'deliberately' hurt other children or adults in order to 'get back at' or provoke staff. On the positive side the pupil may try to provoke surprise or, at a more sophisticated level, do things which provoke laughter. These behaviours fall within the definition of communication. The pupil is doing something with the interest of affecting another person, in an immediate face-to-face situation, in which he or she shows understanding of the reactions of the other person.

Factor analyses of items in this group of communicative behaviours throw light on the development of skills and give clues on programme development. We had thought that we may find groups of pupils using different modes of communication, vocal, gestural and through pictures. In practice the data suggested that there was one general factor of communicative skill. Examination of individual protocols showed that what was important was not the mode but the type of communicative act. If a pupil used sound to express needs they typically also used gesture or pictures as well. Nonetheless the pupil might, for clear physical reasons or because of a generalised failure to develop speech attributable to brain dysfunction, show a greater facility for use of non-vocal than vocal means of communication. The data suggest a mode of early development in which the child learns that he or she can get needs satisfied or prevent interference and then uses whatever method is taught in specific situations, or whatever is learned by chance, to satisfy needs.

The other factor that emerged consistently concerned negative interaction. A small group of pupils showed what were often high levels of negative provocative behaviour. Our analyses indicated that they were often able young people, judged in terms of their comprehension skills and their ability to imitate. They were showing this pattern of interaction as an apparent manifestation of negative attitudes to other people.

Understanding

Three sections of the PVCS assess understanding of non-vocal communication, vocalisation and speech, and emotion. It is clearly important to have an assessment of understanding available in developing a communication programme. Two distinct patterns may emerge. The pupil may score well on comprehension and very poorly on all sections concerned with communication. In this case it would seem reasonable to argue that programmes need to concentrate on an expressive mode, signs or symbols, with speech being seen as the major receptive mode. Or the pupil may show both poor expressive and poor receptive skills. In this case we might want to look at performance in the context of an overall assessment of intelligence or early cognitive development. Uzgiris and Hunt (1975) base their procedures on Piaget's account of the sensori-motor period, between birth and two years. If communication skills are well down in terms of cognitive skills, for example if the pupil shows minimal evidence of receptive or expressive skills but a mental age equivalent of three years, and deafness is ruled out as a cause of delay, then the pupil may be affected by an aphasic-like condition involving a specific language disorder. Evidence from work with aphasic pupils suggests that sign languages, coupled with speech, may be very valuable in giving them both receptive and expressive skills and may, eventually, lead to the acquisition of speech (Kiernan and Reid, 1984).

The pupil with poor cognitive skills, and poor receptive and expressive skills, presents different problems. Here the temptation is to write the pupil off as developmentally delayed overall and to suggest that he or she will develop speech 'when he is ready'. This do-nothing philosophy is not really justifiable. We have already pointed out that communication develops before speech. Furthermore, communication skills clearly facilitate social interaction and, arguably, cognitive development. Finally, communication through sign and symbol is easier to teach then speech, largely because signs and symbol indication can be prompted. For the less able pupil, the communication component would sensibly comprise teaching an augmentative system through which the pupil could initially understand requests, express needs and preferences.

Formal communication

The final section of the PVCS covers the use of formal means of communication, words, signs or symbols. Quite a number of the pupils within our sample had words or signs but often these were used in a non-communicative way. Typically a pupil might 'have' a dozen words or signs, which he or she could produce on demand, but never use them to ask for or spontaneously indicate their referents. Programming for such pupils clearly needs to concentrate on making words or signs relevant within the network of a pupil's needs and interests.

Categories of communicative acts

The initial analyses completed on data from the PVCS suggested that the mode of communication, vocalisations versus gestures and so on, was not significant in grouping pupils. What seemed

60

to be important was the type of communicative act. Further analyses suggested that there were six categories of items. The first three categories all represent fairly basic communication. One category of items reflects simple attention-seeking for its own sake, reaching out to be lifted or approaching to get attention with no follow-up of requesting objects or services. The second category reflects behaviours leading to need satisfaction, 'give me' or 'can I have'. Category three reflects simple negation, 'no, I don't want'. These three categories occurred singly or together in many protocols. In other words there was no evidence suggesting a developmental sequence. However, there was such evidence differentiating these three categories from the next three: pupils who scored well on categories one to three often scored well on the next three, but there were no instances of pupils scoring well on categories four, five or six and scoring poorly on one to three.

The more complex categories cover behaviours where the pupil called attention to objects, people or events simply to share attention, that is without wanting to satisfy a need. Another category covers a rather heterogeneous group of items which seem all to reflect positive interaction patterns which have been learned, like giving things to people, waving goodbye, expressing affection through conventional means or taking turns. The last category covers the provocative behaviours which we commented on earlier. Pupils showing a high level of negative interaction clearly need programmes which are aimed to reduce these 'problem behaviours' by replacing them with acceptable means of expressing emotion. More importantly, they need to be encouraged to build up positive relationships with other people, to learn that interaction can be rewarding and pleasurable.

SCORING AND USING THE PVCS

We have discussed the rationale of the PVCS and the various components. The PVCS was designed as a tool for programme planning. As we noted earlier, it often serves to elicit and organise information which teachers and others already have. The scoring of the full PVCS allows users to summarise information on physical abilities and existing modes of communication which can lead to decisions on the receptive and expressive

61

modes to be used in a programme. Scoring in terms of categories allows decisions on the type of communicative act to be exploited in the teaching of formal systems, or systems which are of more public use than initial methods of communication and the teaching of more complex communicative acts.

DISCUSSION

The teaching of communication skills is as yet a poorly developed part of the curriculum in schools for pupils with severe learning difficulties. The PVCS aims to provide an assessment which can be used to develop programmes to fill a gap at the initial level of such teaching. It was developed against a background of teaching which, in our view, concentrated overmuch on teacher-directed activities concerned with comprehension and naming tasks. A programme developed from the PVCS should provide a greater opportunity for pupils to express their needs, both in a positive way — 'I want that' — and in a negative way — 'no, I don't want that' — and should also focus attention on more complex interactional skills.

The PVCS still leaves massive gaps in coverage at more sophisticated levels of communication. Kiernan (1985), in reviewing evidence from reseach on the communication and language skills of people with mental handicap, points out that more able people may have reasonably good discourse skills but may not use them because of their perceived social status as individuals who are directed and controlled by powerful authority figures such as teachers or therapists. Kiernan suggests that, at a teaching level, much can be learned from the methods developed in teaching second languages or communicative language teaching.

The PVCS was carefully developed as an assessment procedure. We tried to ensure content validity by discussing coverage with practitioners during the initial stages of development. The reliability study was important and illuminating. It is clearly necessary to establish that different people scoring the schedule for the same pupil will agree on the interpretation of items. There were some instances where agreement was low, for example in saying whether a pupil could recognise visual cues or whether they would hover for attention or use looking as a means of communication. Procedures which do not have established reliabilities run the risk of introducing confusion in planning at the first stage of programme development.

The validity study was equally essential. In this study we asked respondents to describe examples of the behaviour of pupils which had led them to check items in the schedule. These descriptions were then rated by three raters in terms of the correspondence of the behaviour described and the intention of the item. Several items were shown to be consistently misinterpreted, including items relating to 'drawing attention' without asking for objects, and one relating to delayed imitation. These items were either rewritten or dropped. Although only a handful of items were consistently misinterpreted, the study made the point that such problems could emerge and that validity needed to be checked.

The development of communication skills is central to the social, emotional and cognitive development of pupils in schools dealing with severe learning difficulties. The PVCS represents one procedure which should help in programme formulation for non-verbal and minimally verbal pupils. However, there is a great need for in-service training which reflects developing knowledge of theory and teaching strategies. Reviews by McLean and Snyder-McLean (1978), Bloom and Lahey (1978) and Kiernan (1985) provide a starting point for increased understanding. A practically orientated text by McCartney (1984) and a book by Kiernan, Reid and Goldbart (1987), based on a workshop, bring the theoretical material and discussion of teaching strategies together in a form which is more accessible to practitioners.

Assessment, although important, only represents one aspect of what needs to be developed. Teachers need to be helped to think through the implications of assessment for teaching, and schools to reorientate their thinking to accommodate new approaches. Without these developments the teaching of communication skills will remain underdeveloped and sadly sterile.

4

Communication for a Purpose

Juliet Goldbart

In the preceding chapters, much of the discussion has involved the assessment of children or adults at very early stages in the development of communication and suggestions about the content of intervention programmes appropriate to their needs. However, this chapter is concerned rather more with the *how* than the *what* of teaching communication skills. In other words, we will try to address some of the ideas and approaches we have found useful in developing the skills and strategies a student needs to transmit successfully some message to another person or persons.

In the discussion in Chapter 1 of the sociolinguistic approach to language acquisition it was argued that children will only learn to use language if they have a reason to do so; that is, if they have something about which to communicate. We extrapolated from this a general principle which underpins our whole approach to intervention: we are more likely to be successful in teaching an adult or child to communicate if what we teach is useful or serves a purpose for that individual, in other words, if what we teach is *functional.*

To see whether this approach to teaching is embodied in currently available approaches to language intervention we need to examine recent sources and materials. The majority of commercially available language teaching kits and programmes and language intervention studies published in the last 20 years are based on the language acquisition theories of either Chomsky (the grammarian account) or Skinner (the behaviourist account), or a combination of the two (Goldbart, 1985; Harris, 1984a). Where both approaches were employed, teaching techniques were usually influenced by the behavioural

approach and the selection of target behaviours by the grammarian approach. Both of these approaches have been criticised
for their focus on theory and their neglect of actual child
language data in their development of theories of language
acquisition (McLean and Snyder-McLean, 1978). It was
claimed in Chapter 1 that these intervention approaches had not
proved to be particularly successful. We now need to look at
that claim and the studies themselves in more detail.

From the mid 1960s to the late 1970s, a considerable
number of papers on language intervention with children with a
wide range of difficulties were published. These covered children with hearing loss (Bennett, 1973), language delay (Hedge
and Gierut, 1979; Leonard, 1974), language disorder (Gray
and Fygetakis, 1968; Zwitman and Sonderman, 1979), autism
(Carr, Schreibman and Lovaas, 1975; Hargrave and Swisher,
1975) and severe mental handicap (Bricker and Bricker, 1974;
Halle, Marshall and Spradlin, 1979). We will concern ourselves
mainly with those involving children diagnosed as either autistic
or severely mentally handicapped.

Despite great differences in the behaviourist (Skinnerian)
approach and the grammarian (Chomskian) approaches to
language acquisition, the majority of the intervention studies
based on these approaches have certain features in common.
The first point to strike the reader is that the focus of interest of
the whole intervention is often on what happens in the immediate teaching context. This can be seen by looking at the extent
to which these studies look for generalisation to spontaneous
use; that is, whether targets which are achieved during teaching
are subsequently used outside the teaching context. In only 59.8
per cent of 39 studies of autistic children, 58.3 per cent of
twelve studies of children with language disorder, language
delay or hearing loss and 36.4 per cent of 55 studies of children
with severe mental handicap was an attempt made to see
whether generalisation had been achieved (Goldbart, 1985).
This difference between studies of children with mental handicap and those with non-mentally handicapped subjects suggests
that researchers working with mentally handicapped subjects
had lower expectations of generalisation than those working
with other subjects.

Even in those studies which have been influenced by the
grammarian perspective, the teaching techniques are drawn
mainly from behaviour modification. These techniques include

shaping, modelling and imitation, prompting and fading, forward and backward chaining and training and the use of tangible reinforcers. Whilst such techniques are highly applicable to much teaching, in particular within a special education framework (Porter, 1986), the way they have been used in language teaching tends to limit the opportunities for conversational interchange and true communication. Typically, the teacher or therapist presents a verbal and/or a visual (such as a picture or object) stimulus and the learner is required to produce a predetermined response, often a label, for example: 'What's this?' 'Drink', 'Yes, drink'. Thus, there is a non-maintenance of communication. There is not very far you can go with that conversation!

If we examine the reinforcement used in many of these studies, there is often little relation between the reinforcer used and the language being taught, for example: 'What's this?' 'Drink', 'Yes, drink'; reinforcement — a piece of apple.

Even if social praise is used as a reinforcer, the options for conversation are limited: 'What's this?' 'Ball', 'Yes, *good talking*!' What is the appropriate 'next turn' in this conversation?

There seems, furthermore, to be an excessive concern with the teaching of object labels. This assumes that once the learner has acquired a particular word for a particular use, it will automatically be used in all other relevant contexts. For example, if we teach the student to label a cup as 'drink', this will subsequently be used for requesting a drink, commenting that another student has a drink and telling someone else to finish their drink. We do not have evidence that this is true of delayed or impaired language learners, and, as Mittler and Berry (1977) suggest, this excessive teaching of object labels may in fact negatively affect language learning.

Selection of target behaviours is determined by the perspective of language acquisition adopted by the researcher. In the case of a Skinnerian approach, this is usually by task-analysing a word. For example: to teach 'mummy', the child is taught to say the sounds *m, u* and *y*, these are then chained together to make 'mummy'. It is hard to envisage how the learner is to make the connection between this string of sounds and, for example, the person who puts them to bed at night.

Despite what we may expect, the Chomskian approach, with its emphasis on grammatical structures did not always lead to a more sensible selection of targets. For example, the emphasis on teaching object labels, which will be discussed further in the following chapter. Furthermore, since English is a notoriously irregular language, attempts to highlight grammatical categories sometimes created major difficulties for researchers. For instance, it would have been confusing to teach irregular past tense forms. Hence 'This is the baker, today he bakes, yesterday he baked. This is the flier, today he flies, yesterday he flied'!

By 1978, the success of these studies in facilitating the development of language and communication was being questioned. For example, Guess, Keogh and Sailor (1978), who had invested much time and energy in such studies, were saying: 'Little is known about the extent to which spontaneous functional language can be taught to mentally handicapped children', and Rutter (1980), in relation to children with autism: 'It is clear from a host of studies that operant treatments have often been followed by improved speech production, but have they specifically influenced the development of language in the sense of a symbolic code that allows the generation of normal messages?' It seems, therefore, that despite a large number of studies, no clearly successful route to increasing spontaneous language and communication had been established.

As a response, and as a result of research on language acquisition in normally developing children, the last five years have seen several attempts to approach language intervention in a more ecologically valid way (Campbell and Stremel-Campbell, 1986; Martin, McConkey and Martin, 1984). These studies have been concerned with making more use of the language learner's social environment and drawing more on what is known about normally developing children's language acquisition and communicative interactions. To do this we need to know more about the existing language environments of delayed or impaired communicators. The studies of interactions between people with mental handicap and others in their environment fall into three categories; studies of parents and their young children, of teachers and students in the classroom and of mentally handicapped adults and staff in residential settings.

There is some controversy surrounding research on the language input of mothers to their young mentally handicapped children. Rondal (1976) finds that, in most respects, the language of mothers to their Down's syndrome children is the

67

same as that of mothers to normally developing children matched to the Down's syndrome children on mean length of utterance. However, Rondal, like some other researchers, finds some minor differences, and this area would benefit from further detailed research.

There are two studies of classroom interactions, which yield quite similar results. The first is by Beveridge and Hurrell (1980), who recorded teachers' responses to 2,000 initiations from four children in each of ten severe learning difficulty (SLD) classes. The responses they observed are given in Table 4.1, and it can be seen that the most common responses that the children receive are 'brief acknowledgement', 'ignoring' and 'simple immediate response'. Within these interactions, therefore, there is very little that is going to maintain conversation. The only category which seems to be truly facilitative in terms of providing an opportunity for teaching or practising language or communication is 'verbalisation expanding the child's idea or content' which is the response to about one in six of the children's initiations.

Similarly, Goldbart (1985) looking at school-age children with severe learning difficulties, and pre-schoolers with and without severe learning difficulties (five in each group), recorded the number and success of initiations directed by children to classroom staff in a time period. Successful initiations were those after which the child received undivided attention from the adult. (The figures are presented in Table 4.2.) Although the differences are not large, the children with severe learning difficulties appear to initiate less frequently and less successfully than normally developing pre-schoolers.

A study of young mentally handicapped adults in a hospital setting by Prior et al (1979) had similar results. They found that staff used instruction-type language most frequently and conversation-type language least frequently. Again, there was a high frequency of staff ignoring initiations from residents. Similarly, Pratt, Blumstead and Raynes' (1976) study of a large institution for mentally handicapped adults showed that staff talking to residents used controlling language more often than informative language. This is important because Tizard et al (1972) found that speech types defined as informative were better for residents' language development than those defined as controlling.

All these studies suggest that if we want to promote the kind

Table 4.1: Teachers' responses to children's initiations

Responses which non-maintained the interaction		Responses which maintained the interaction	
Ignoring: not seeing/hearing initiation: no response	23.3%	Simple immediate response, inviting further interaction, eg 'Yes' or 'Good'	20.3%
Brief acknowledgement but then moves away or redirects attention	33.4%	Verbalisation expanding child's idea or content	15.6%
Negative verbalisation: 'Stop it', 'Go away'	1.7%	Verbalisation changing child's idea or content	1.5%
No verbalisation and interaction not maintained, but positive gesture or action	2.8%	Continuous referral, eg 'Come and show me when you've done it'	0.5%
Negative nonverbal, eg smack or rough removal of an object	0.05%	Non-verbal but positive action or gesture which maintains the interaction, eg joins in game, smiles	0.85%

(Adapted from Beveridge and Hurrell, 1980)

Table 4.2: Number and success of initiations by children towards adults

Children	No. I	No. and % I*
Preschool SLD	79	19 (24.05%)
School age SLD	79	20 (25.32%)
'Normal' pre-school	91	36 (39.56%)

I = Initiation directed to adult
I* = Initiation receiving undivided adult attention
Adapted from Goldbart, 1985

of interactions which we know to facilitate language development in normally developing children, we need to think about ways of restructuring the interactions between people with impaired communication skills and their teachers and caregivers. This would necessitate two areas of planning. First, that the target behaviours identified for individuals' language and communication programmes and the contexts chosen for teaching must reflect the purposes for which language is used. A second aim must be to engineer more opportunities for children and adults with severe learning difficulties to experience the kind of interactions normally developing toddlers have with their caregivers. This would include more opportunities to affect and control their environment. In order to do these things, we need to know the purposes to which language is put, in particular in interactions between young or impaired communicators and others. What do we need to be able to *do* with the communication skills we have? How can these functions of communication be best portrayed?

In the previous chapter, Kiernan demonstrated the communicative functions which can be identified as part of the PVCS assessment. These provide a useful way of identifying what an individual can do with the skills he or she has. Similar sets of categories have been established by Halliday (1975) in his study of one child's development (see Table 4.3) and by Cirrin and Rowland (1985) in their study of adolescents with severe learning difficulties. There is considerable agreement among the three sets of categories as shown in Table 4.4 (for further discussion see Kiernan, Reid and Goldbart, 1987). Definitions of Halliday's functions are given in Table 4.3. Kiernan and Reid's have been explained in the preceding chapter and Cirrin and Rowland's should be self-explanatory.

Table 4.3: Halliday's (1975) functions form 'Learning How to Mean'

Instrumental	— satisfying one's needs
Regulatory	— controlling other's behaviour
Interaction	— you and me, greetings, names
Personal	— awareness of self
Heuristic	— seeking information
Imaginative	— pretend and make believe
Informative	— telling others things

The first four functions develop before the later three.

There are obviously many similarities between the three lists in Table 4.4. Kiernan and Reid's and Cirrin and Rowland's have the advantage of having been developed in relation to people with severe learning difficulties, but Halliday's extends into

Table 4.4: Communicative functions according to the different authors

Kiernan and Reid (1987 a&b)	Cirrin and Rowland (1985)	Halliday (1975)
Seeking attention	Directs attention to self	Personal
Need satisfaction	Requests object	Instrumental
Need satisfaction	Requests action	Regulatory
Simple negation	Protest	Personal
Positive interaction	Directs attention for communication	Interactional
Negative interaction	—	—
Shared attention	Directs attention to object	Regulatory/Informational
—	Requests information	Heuristic
—	Answers	—
—	—	Imaginative

rather more advanced communicative functions. If we want impaired communicators to develop truly effective communication skills they will need to have the opportunity to communicate, at least, all the functions described by Kiernan and Reid. The need to restructure the environments of people with severe learning difficulties, as outlined above, is part of this process.

In many ways, the 'well-run' classroom is not a good place to learn to communicate or to affect your environment. Apart from the points outlined above, children are provided with food at meal-times, and a drink at break-time, children are all taken to the toilet, put on the potty or changed at regular intervals, play equipment is changed regularly, and children are not allowed to remain at one activity for too long. Each child is engaged in short periods of intensive one-to-one teaching or group work and periods of free play, as appropriate to their needs.

What need is there to communicate?

So, teachers, therapists and researchers have been thinking about general strategies for trying to improve opportunities for real communication in the classroom or training centre, in particular, communication to have an effect on the environment. Hence, as Seibert and Oller (1981) say: 'the primary goal of intervention becomes the facilitation of generalised communicative functions for which syntactic structure and semantic

content are only the tools'. The case for this type of intervention, with particular emphasis on children and adolescents
using at least a few words, has been well argued by Bell (1985),
Harris (1984b), Newton (1981) and Snyder-McLean et al
(1984). The latter three studies also include some evaluation of
their proposals.

GENERAL STRATEGIES FOR PROMOTING COMMUNICATION

(1) Giving students the opportunity to express real *choices,
needs* or *preferences*. For example, offering the student a choice
between milk and orange juice, or asking 'which apple do you
want?' The response to this could be a reach or other simple
gesture, with or without a vocalisation, or it could be more
sophisticated, for example the name of the preferred item or
'That!'

Chris, an independently mobile eight-year-old with severe
learning difficulties, shows very limited skills in either 'seeking
attention' or 'need satisfaction' on the pre-verbal communication assessment. He has been given opportunities to choose
between toys and items of food and drink by reaching towards
and making contact with the hand which is holding the thing he
wants. Physical prompting has been necessary, but this is now a
fairly well-established means of communication.

(2) Giving students the opportunity to *request* or *refuse* objects
or events. For example, asking the student: 'Do you want to go
to the toilet?', or offering the option of moving on to another
type of activity or more of an activity which they have just tried.
Again, the response could be a gesture and/or a vocalisation, it
could be a change in orientation or facial expression, or an eye-
point.

Louise, for instance, demonstrates a wide range of interpretable responses on the Affective Communication Assessment,
and is just starting to communicate intentionally. However, she
is severely limited physically. Thus, a frown plus puckering of
her lips indicates that she does not want a drink of water.

(3) Setting up unpredictable events, or arranging the non-
occurrence of normally reliable events, within a familiar and
well understood routine, which gives the student the opportun-

ity to *comment* on or *communicate* with others about something unexpected. For example, breaking the tips off classroom pencils, taking the middle pin out of a pair of scissors, handing round an empty biscuit tin, giving a student an empty jug and asking him or her to pour drinks for everyone.

Aysha, for instance, is asked to pour a drink for other members of her class at snack time. But the jug is empty. She attempts to pour from the jug, quickly notices that nothing is coming out, then looks into the jug. She hands the jug back to her teacher shaking her head and saying 'Gone!'

(4) Setting up opportunities for *problem solving* by individuals or groups. This problem solving might require the use of cognitive strategies only on the part of the student, or may involve communication with others about how the problem is to be solved. For example, the student is given the opportunity to obtain a desired object which is within sight but out of reach. Clues can be provided, a chair to stand on or a stick to extend reach. Or three students together are asked to take an inflated paddling-pool out of the classroom to the playground. Since the paddling pool is wider than the door, the three will have to work out between them a strategy for getting it out.

Bobby's teacher (Sue Walker, see Chapter 5) wants him to solve a problem; she will help him if asked. The task is to retrieve a biscuit which is out of reach, on a chair which is on top of a table. The teacher asks who would like to get it, Bobby puts up his hand as a request to be the agent and is given a stick. Having attempted to reach the biscuit whilst standing on the floor, he then positions and climbs on his own chair. With the stick he pushes the biscuit off the chair, but, unfortunately, it falls on the floor. Bobby's teacher offers him another biscuit. He refuses this by shaking his head, then takes it, places it back on the seat of the chair. Then, using the stick, he retrieves it successfully.

In our experience these situations are highly motivating and greatly enjoyed, to the extent that it is not uncommon for students who successfully complete a task by accident to indicate that they want to do it again 'properly'.

(5) Setting up and participating in *joint action routines* (Snyder-McLean et al, 1984). This approach draws on the findings of both the psycholinguistic approach and the sociolinguistic approach and, hence, provides a bridge to the following

chapter. Joint action routines are formulated play routines which can be built around everyday events like dressing or having a bath, or play routines like pretend tea parties, taking turns with simple toys or very sophisticated routines like rescuing someone from a burning house. In many ways they parallel the pretend play or role-play sequences engaged in by normally developing pre-schoolers. Like a lot of pretend play, joint action routines have set routines with opportunities for variation, a plot or purpose and scope for a variety of different roles. They can be adult devised so that opportunities for expressing a range of communicative functions can be built in. Hence, the child gains experience in communicating in different roles, for different purposes, but within a clearly understood familiar framework with an adult model when needed.

While these ideas can be used at very early stages, for example, in a turn-taking game, rolling a ball from adult to child and back again, with each participant simply communicating their readiness for the next turn, they can obviously be used in complex settings requiring complex language. They are included here, at least in part, to show how these ideas can be extended forwards to children or adults at higher stages of communicative development. The following is a transcript of an excerpt from a joint action routine involving the author and two young boys, David and Gavin. Both boys were using a number of gestures for communicating and one or two single words.

Joint Action Routine: Putting dolly to bed.
JG. Look! Here's dolly. (Shows doll to both boys).
JG. She's going to have a bath.
(Gavin points to the bath and looks to JG for confirmation)
JG. Yes, in there,
JG. Who's going to take off trousers?
(Gavin and David point to themselves.)
JG. David take off trousers! Pull, pull, pull!
(David takes off trousers while Gavin watches.)
JG. Who's going to take off jumper?
(Gavin reaches for doll, takes off jumper while David watches.)
JG. Jumper off, good boy.
(Gavin holds naked doll.)
JG. Where's she going?
(Gavin puts doll in the bath, looks up for confirmation.)

JG. In the bath. (Nods to Gavin.)
(Gavin turns doll round to face him.)
JG. What are you going to wash? (Models action of washing.)
(Gavin rubs hands together, David imitates.)
JG. Oh! Wash hands, yes, wash hands.
(Gavin looks up, reaches for flannel.)
JG. Want flannel? (Gives him flannel.)
(Gavin washes doll's hands.)
JG. Now David's turn
(Gavin passes doll and bath to David a little unwillingly.)
(David takes flannel and washes the doll's face and head.)
JG. What are you washing?
(David rubs his hands over his hair.)
JG. Yes, hair, wash hair.

The examples given for these strategies are ones we have found useful, mainly in a school setting. Readers will need to consider how they may be altered or adapted to fit the settings in which they work. The PVCS (see previous chapter) has been found to be useful in suggesting appropriate ways of using the general strategies, for example in suggesting the means of communication used and possible reinforcing contexts. Parents, teachers and other staff, knowing their children or the people they work with will have many other ideas which are functional, real opportunities for communication, and fit naturally in to the daily routine. One important issue in relation to working with adults with mental handicap is that it is often thought the use of toys or miniatures is not age-appropriate and, hence, the type of input needed for language development may not be provided. Joint action routines can be built around everyday activities like washing up, shopping, dressing and meal times, so they can be planned and carried out very successfully with adults in adult training centres, social education centres and residential settings (Jones, 1986).

Finally, for some students establishing the idea of communication will be the whole aim of intervention for some time, while for others a wide range of communicative functions can be taught in this way. There will be students with good communication skills in certain settings, for whom these ideas may provide a means of generalising these already learned behaviours to a much wider range of contexts.

5

Teaching First Meanings

Judith Coupe, Linda Barton and Sue Walker

This chapter describes a method of teaching early meanings to pupils who demonstrate a range of appropriate actions with objects, and who understand and communicate about objects and events within their environment.

Early meanings are defined by Leonard (1984) as 'aspects of cognitive structure that the child may attempt to communicate about'. First meanings, therefore, are concerned with people, objects and events which are familiar to the child in the final stage of sensori-motor development — (as discussed in Chapter 1). For Bloom (1973) the earliest of these meanings were: existence of entities; non-existence of items children expect to find; disappearance of things. Our approach to teaching first meanings was developed in the light of results of a language survey carried out at Melland School (Coupe, 1981) when 28.4 per cent of pupils were at or below the stage of imitating single words. This agreed closely with the results of the Schools Council Survey (Leeming et al, 1979) and the work of Kiernan, Reid and Jones (1982). It seemed that many pupils were failing to develop functional communication at the single word level. Hence, we examined the content and approach of existing teaching methods and determined that, due to a lack of accessible and sensitive research and intervention strategies, the teaching of comprehension and expression of single words tended to emphasise the use of nouns to identity objects and pictures. Mittler and Berry (1977) suggest that this undue emphasis on the teaching of labelling may be counterproductive to language development.

Whilst object names do constitute a high proportion of the

first words young children use (Benedict, 1979 — 50 per cent; Nelson, 1973 — 51 per cent), intervention strategies seemed to neglect the meanings conveyed, that is semantic roles, and the uses intended, that is the functions of these single words. Thus, the underlying concepts were generally not taught and there was a lack of emphasis on teaching language skills in a communicative context. (See Chapter 4 for further details.) Recent research into the language acquisition of normally developing children demonstrates that the earliest words and protowords used by the children are usefully classified according to the semantic role, that is the underlying meaning of the utterance as opposed to its grammatical category or its function. (Greenfield and Smith, 1976; Leonard, 1984; Nelson, 1973). In view of the range of semantic roles described in these studies, it seemed likely that pupils with severe learning difficulties have delayed or deficient development of semantic notions which, therefore, requires specific remediation. In the light of this rationale we developed the following three perspectives (Barton and Coupe, 1985):

(1) Teach first meanings concepts rather than verbal labels.

(2) Place teaching in a setting where each child has something to communicate about.

(3) Provide opportunities for children who are not yet ready to use words to communicate intentionally with gestures, vocalisations and protowords. This would follow the normal development sequence described in Chapter 1. Bates, Camaioni and Volterra (1975) tentatively suggest that gestural and vocal signals gradually give way to increasingly wordlike sounds before the use of verbal symbols at sensori-motor stages 5-6.

FIRST MEANINGS

We chose to teach the early meanings described below, which were influenced by the work of Bloom (1973), Bloom and Lahey (1978) and Leonard (1984).

Existence

The child acknowledges that an object or event exists by look, gesture, vocalisation, sign or word. For example, when presented with a doll, the child reaches and touches it then looks to the adult.

Disappearance

The child comments or requests the disappearance of a person or object by look, gesture, vocalisation, sign or word, such as 'no', 'gone' or 'away'. For example, when a toy car is pushed into a garage, the child gestures with upturned hands.

Recurrence

The child comments on or requests a representation of an object that existed but disappeared, or a repetition of an action that occurred then stopped, either non-verbally by a point, gesture, vocalisation, or by a word or sign such as 'again', or 'more'. For example a battery-operated car is activated by an adult. The child looks at the adult and vocalises to request a repetition of the action.

Non-existence

The child indicates that an object does not exist where he expects it to be, either non-verbally by a look, gesture, or vocalisation, or by a word or sign such as 'no', 'gone', or the name of an object. For example, a child is given an empty biro and told to draw. Lack of results leads to showing of the pen and 'tuts'.

Location

The child comments on the position of an object, person or event or the spatial relationship between two objects, or requests that an object is placed in a certain location by look, gesture, vocalisation, or a word or sign such as 'there', 'on', 'table'. For example, the child's coat is on another child's coat peg. The child visually searches, sees her own coat, looks at the adult and points to her coat.

Possession

The child conveys the relationship between an object or/person and themselves or another, by a look, gesture, vocalisation, sign or word such as 'mine'. For example, the child points to herself when asked 'Whose coat is this?'.

Rejection

The child communicates that he does not want an object, adult or event, or that he wants an activity to cease by a look, gesture, vocalisation, or a sign or word such as 'no', 'stop', 'bye bye', 'gone'. For example, a child is offered sticky play dough. He looks at it, touches it and then pushes away the adult hand that is holding it.

Denial

The child denies a proposition by look, gesture, vocalisation, or a word or sign such as 'no', or 'didn't'. For example, a child takes a crisp when the adult is not looking. The adult accuses the child who, with a full mouth, shakes her head.

Agent

This is the person or object that causes an action to occur. The child can convey this by a look, gesture, or vocalisation, or a word or sign. For example, on presentation of a jug of orange juice and glasses the child points to himself and says 'me', to indicate that he wants to pour.

Object

This is the object or person that may be affected by an action. The child can convey this by look, gesture, or vocalisation, or a word or sign. For example, when shown a toothbrush, the child points to her teeth and says, 'teeth'.

Action

This is any observable activity or change of state. The child can express this non-verbally by a look, gesture or vocalisation or by a word or sign such as 'up', 'go', 'jump'. For example, when offered some pop-up cones, the child says, 'go' and presses the lever to make them work.

Attribute

The child comments on or requests a property of an object or person by look, gesture, vocalisation or a word or sign such as 'big', 'hot', 'horrid', or 'nice'. For example, the child wets his pants, points to his pants and comments, 'wet'.

PRE-REQUISITES TO TEACHING FIRST MEANINGS

We have determined three important pre-requisites for the teaching of first meanings:

Cognitive

The pupil should be functioning at the end of sensori-motor stage 4 and entering into stage 5 in the following scales.
(1) Means for obtaining desired environmental events.
(2) Object-related schemes.
(3) Visual pursuit and permanence of objects.
To determine the developmental stage of an individual pupil, see Coupe and Levy (1985), Dunst (1980) and Uzgiris and Hunt (1975).

Communicative

The pupil should have acquired intentional communication by gesture, looking or vocalisation. There should be evidence of an object concept and actions on objects.

Social interactional

The pupils should be capable of having their attention directed by adults in giving joint attention to events and objects.

TEACHING FIRST MEANINGS — AN EXAMPLE LESSON

The following transcript is of a lesson with five nursery age pupils and two staff, a teacher and speech therapist. The sequence of meanings taught was:
(1) Existence: a toy car is presented and is acknowledged by each child.
(2) Agent: who wants to make the car go?
(3) Action: the agent makes the car go.
(4) Recurrence: the agent controls for the action to be repeated.
(5) Action: the agent makes the car go.
First, the teacher modelled the play sequence with the toy car, emphasising the meanings involved. Children were then given the opportunity to nominate themselves as the agent. So that Christopher, for instance, pointed to himself and vocalised that he wanted his turn in acting upon the car. He took it from the teacher, put it on the floor and, after verbal prompting from the teacher, pushed it along the floor. When the teacher retrieved the car, he requested recurrence of the sequence by saying, 'Again'. He then repeated the sequence. On completion of Christopher's turn the teacher allowed opportunity for other children to nominate themselves as agent. Careful recording by the speech therapist ensured that all the children's communicative responses were noted.

In this lesson, whilst the teacher worked with the pupils, the speech therapist recorded their behaviour. Of necessity, a quick and easy format of recording is required. However, when possible, we do advocate that lessons are regularly videoed so that more detailed recording and identification of pupils' progress can be made from the tape. The sequence of meanings is noted and the child behaviours are then recorded as they occur in sequence. The objects used should be varied with repetition of the sequence so that, in this instance, after teaching the planned sequence of meanings with a toy car, the lesson was repeated using a ball and skittles.

Teacher

Existence	Teacher holds up car
	Teacher says, 'Car ... look, look, look'
	Teacher puts car on floor
	Teacher says, 'Look'
Action	Teacher pushes car and says, 'Go'
Recurrence	Teacher picks up car, holds up, says 'Again'
Action	Teacher pushes car and says, 'Go'

Christopher

Existence	Teacher holds up car
	Christopher *looks* at car
Agent	Teacher asks, 'Who wants it?'
	Christopher *points to self* and *vocalises*
	Teacher says, 'Good boy, Chris', gives him car
	Christopher takes car, puts it on floor
Action	Teacher says, 'Go'
	Christopher pushes car
Recurrence	Teacher picks up car and holds it up
	Christopher takes car and *vocalises* an approximation to 'Again'
Action	Teacher responds by saying, 'Again, good boy'
	Christopher pushes car
	Teacher says, 'Go' and catches car

Natalie

Existence	Teacher holds car
	Natalie *looks*
Agent	Teacher asks, 'Who wants it?'
	Natalie *vocalises* and *points to self* (gesture)
	Teacher says, 'Good girl', puts car in Natalie's hand.
	Natalie drops car
Action	Teacher retrieves car and says, 'Go'
	Natalie prompted to push car
Recurrence	Teacher picks up car, holds it in front of Natalie

Natalie *vocalises for more*
Teacher responds, 'Again, good girl'
Action   Teacher puts in Natalie's hand
Natalie prompted to hold car
Teacher says, 'Good girl, Natalie, go'
Natalie pushes car

Martina

Existence	Teacher holds up car
	Martina *looks*
Agent	Teacher asks, 'Who wants it?'
	Martina *vocalises*
	Teacher acknowledges, 'Good girl, Martina'
Action	Teacher gives car to Martina
	Martina takes car
	Teacher says, 'Go'
	Martina prompted to push it
Recurrence	Teacher picks up car, places it in Martina's hand, asks, 'Again?'
Action	Martina with prompting, *pushes the car*
	Teacher picks up car, looks at Martina, says, 'Good girl'

Joseph

Existence	Teacher shows car
	Joseph *looks*
Agent	Teacher asks, 'Who wants it?'
	Joseph *vocalises*
	Teacher repeats to Joseph, 'Who wants a go?'
	Joseph *prompted to point to self* and spontaneously says, '*Me*'
	Teacher touches his face, says, 'Good boy'
Action	Teacher gives Joseph the car
	Teacher says, 'Go'
	Joseph places the car on the floor and pushes
Recurrence	Teacher retrieves the car, says, 'Again'
	Joseph retrieves the car and has a second quick go

Action	Teacher says, 'Go'
	Joseph takes car and pushes it
	Teacher picks up car and says, 'Good boy'

Emma

Agent	Emma calls out, '*Me*'
	Teacher responds, 'Good girl, Emma'
	(Teacher talks to scorer)
Action	Teacher gives Emma the car, says 'Ready'
	Emma holds car, says, '*Go*', then turns away from circle to push car
	Teacher comments, 'Ooh' as car stops, then, 'Go and get it'
	Emma goes to retrieve car, taking her time
Recurrence	Teacher says, 'Again Emma, again, again'
	Emma picks up car
Action	Teacher says, 'Go. Go. Hurrah'
	Emma pushes car

CONSIDERATIONS FOR EFFECTIVE TEACHING

Teaching first meanings should be as enjoyable and functionally appropriate as possible within a structured framework which creates maximum opportunity for communication. To provide for this, the following strategies should be considered and utilised.

Management of pupils

For many children, individual teaching can take place in groups the ideal numbers being four to six pupils to two adults. For others it will be more appropriate to work in a smaller group or one to one. We have found it useful to involve a combination of teacher, nursery nurse and speech therapist. The requirements of each lesson need not be the same for each child in the group. In this way, individual needs can be met in terms of level of experience, joint attention, vocalisations, gestures, words, signs and the degree of prompting. Group teaching provides much

84

opportunity for modelling and imitation of other children's behaviour and allows much repetition and practice of meanings. Target behaviours for each pupil can be determined and effectively taught. These will specify what the individual pupil will be expected to do, when, under what conditions and to what criterion of success. (See Chapter 6).

Sequencing meanings

The pupils are involved in simple events which clearly exemplify specific meanings, for example activating toys, hiding themselves or objects, observing the location of objects. These meanings are then sequenced to provide a meaningful routine which the pupils are likely to encounter in their daily experience.

Generalisation

Generalisation of each sequence of meanings is established by using a range of functionally appropriate objects, events, people and locations. For instance, the toy car was used in the demonstration lesson and this was followed by the ball and skittles.

Materials

The same sequence can be repeated using different materials. It is most important to aid the generalisation of the meanings being taught. Materials are important. They need to be carefully selected to be motivating and clearly illustrative of the meaning being taught. After any teaching session materials can be left out to allow children to initiate and practise the sequences amongst themselves.

Presentation

Each meaning must be clearly presented and the language accompanying it should be economical but predetermined and should coincide exactly with the event or function being conveyed.

Reinforcement

Essentially this should be intrinsic. However, for some pupils strong social reinforcement will be a major factor.

Recording and evaluation

It is essential to record pupils' behaviour on a regular basis so that an evaluation can be made of their individual progress. Evaluation will be concerned with the frequency of behaviours but, most importantly, the behaviours themselves and the progression towards spontaneous communication of the meanings. A group recording sheet can be designed which allows for recording of individual pupil's behaviours. The behaviours to note are look, gesture, vocalisation, word and sign. If prompting is required — and this includes imitation of a behaviour — then this should be noted. The same recording sheet can be adapted and used for an individual child.

Recording is important and should be quick and simple to carry out. Sequences of meanings can be approached in two different ways:

(1) An individual child's performance may be recorded in detail whilst they take part in a group lesson.

(2) The performance of all pupils in the group can be recorded as they take their turn during the lesson.

A PRACTICAL APPROACH TO SEQUENCING AND GENERALISING FIRST MEANINGS

The teaching of first meanings is not an end in itself but a foundation upon which to generalise and build communicative strategies and abilities. In both the classroom and the home it is possible to manipulate common, everyday situations and objects so as to teach sequences of meanings in a variety of functionally appropriate contexts. Essentially we wish to see evidence that the child can spontaneously use and understand each concept taught and for this to be generalised to a variety of appropriate contexts.

It is possible for everyday situations to be utilised in order to meet the communicative needs of individual pupils. Martina and Emma are members of an infant class and during their milk break maximum opportunities for communication are created. For Martina, her priority target behaviour for communication stipulates that she will use the first meanings of location, agent, action, recurrence and rejection in the following functionally appropriate situations: milk break, dressing, dolls' house play and fine and gross motor activities. She will use each meaning in the varied situations to a criterion for success of 10/10. Emma's priority target behaviour is similar, but extends to the meanings of location, agent, action, object, non-existence, denial, recurrence, attribute and disappearance.

For the staff or parent it is essential that the individual child is given opportunities to initiate and control for the outcome of a situation — however structured these settings may be. The milk break for this infant class allows individual sequences of meanings to be communicated by all the children daily. Furthermore, it proves to be a naturally social situation which is motivating for the whole class. The following two examples show how milktime creates opportunities for Martina and Emma to communicate.

Martina: First meanings used during milk break

Location	Looks at adult and points to milk on the table.
Agent	Nominates either herself or adult to pour by looking at adult and pouring herself, or looking at adult and placing their hand on the milk bottle. This is usually accompanied by vocalisation.
Action	If Martina pours the milk she usually requires prompts from the adult. If the adult pours she looks at the adult and their action of pouring.
Recurrence	Martina indicates that she wants more by look, vocalisation and a sign.
Rejection	If given water instead of milk, she will push it away and look at the adult.

Emma: First meanings used during milk break

Location	Obtains the milk from the corridor and communicates about its location by pointing outside the classroom, together with, 'There'.
Agent	She indicates that she wants to pour and give the milk out by pointing to herself and saying, 'Me'.
Action	She pours the milk and gives it out, accompanied by eye contact with each child in turn and by saying, 'Here,' or the child's name.
Object	She labels 'milk', 'cup' and 'straw' at appropriate points in the milk-break sequence.
Non-Existence	She communicates if the milk or cups are not in the expected place. Usually by facial expression, look to the adult and sometimes, 'Gone' or 'Not there'.
Denial	If Emma spills the milk whilst pouring, she denies that she did it. Sometimes by answering the accusation with a shake of her head and 'No', and often by pointing to the child closest to her.
Recurrence	Signs and says, 'More' when she wants more milk or 'Again' if she wishes to pour more for other children.
Attribute	She now comments about the attributes of objects. 'Nice' (about the milk) and selects the larger quantity for herself and looks at the adult whilst doing so.
Disappearance	Emma often teases adults or children by hiding a milk bottle or cup behind her back, accompanied by, 'Gone'.

These examples demonstrate how the same context can be readily utilised to build up a varying complexity of sequences appropriate to the developmental level of each child. It is also possible to highlight and teach one specific meaning at a time.

In the same infant class a group of four children were involved in putting their shoes on after a physical education lesson. All the meanings used, apart from denial, were well established and generalised, hence the teacher targeted this particular first meaning. The sequence of meanings consisted of:

(1) Existence: Child acknowledges shoes.

(2) Location: Child locates shoes in different positions.

(3) Denial: Child denies possession of shoes other than their own.

(4) Agent: Child nominates self or adult to put shoes on.

(5) Object; Shows understanding of concept shoe and communicates about it,

(6) Action: Puts shoe on.

The first meaning of denial was, in this instance, taught by the adult giving each child the wrong shoe and also by the adult insisting that the child's shoe was her own. In varying ways, sometimes with prompts, all four children denied possession of another child's shoe and denied the adult possession of children's shoes.

A further example of placing emphasis on one meaning is highlighted within the daily milk-break routine. The children in turn, or in pairs, are given the task of getting their milk but, unknown to them, the milk crate has been removed from its usual place in the corridor. To make functional use of the concept of non-existence the children are required to communicate that the milk is not where it was expected to be. Hajra understands the cognitive concept of non-existence so that, for instance, when the milk crate is not in its expected position she will search other locations to find it. The emphasis of teaching non-existence as a first meaning is to teach her to communicate about this concept. With prompting, when necessary, she was taught to convey the non-existence of the milk. Indeed, during milk break routines over a period of time she was presented with varying situations in which she could generalise and convey the meaning of non-existence. She was given an anticipated cup of milk — with no milk in it. She was asked to get the cups from the shelf but they were not where they should have been.

Like anything else which is to be taught as a priority target behaviour, first meanings should incorporate assessment, programme planning, recording and evaluation (APRE; Coupe, 1986). Through this approach a profile of the child's progress can be established over a period of time. Regular detailed recording of Hajra's functional communication of first meanings (Table 5.1) highlights the progress she has made over two years.

Table 5.1: Record of Hajra's communicative functioning in first meanings

Date	First meaning sequence	Hajra's behaviour
11 June 1984	Existence	—
	Agent	Gesture, look
	Action	Prompted gesture
	Recurrence	—
	Action	Prompted gesture
10 December 1984	Existence	Look
	Agent	Gesture vocalisation
	Action	———
	Recurrence	Look, gesture
	Action	Prompted, gesture
11 February 1985	Existence	Look
	Agent	Gesture, word 'Hajra'
	Action	———
	Recurrence	Look, gesture
	Action	———
10 June 1985	Existence	Look
	Agent	Gesture word 'Hajra'
	Action	Prompted gesture
	Disappearance	Gesture, vocalisation
	Recurrence	Look, gesture, vocalisation
	Action	Prompted gesture
	N.B. Hajra reluctant to carry out action. Relies on being prompted.	
2 December 1985	Existence	Look
	Agent	Gesture, word
	Action	Gesture
	Disappearance	Gesture
	Recurrence	Look, gesture, vocalisation
	Action	Gesture
	N.B. No prompts needed.	
3 February 1986	Existence	Look
	Agent	Gesture, word
	Action	Gesture
	Disappearance	Gesture, vocalisation
	Recurrence	Look, gesture, vocalisation
	Action	Gesture
16 June 1986	Location	Look, gesture, vocalise, word
	Agent	Vocalisation, word, gesture, look
	Action	Gesture, look, vocalisation, word
	Non-existence	Prompted look, gesture, vocalisation
	Existence	Gesture, look, vocalisation

By June 1986, Hajra was using a full repertoire of behaviours to communicate about the first meanings she has been taught. Furthermore, she was able to generalise these meanings to a wide range of functions and events.

CONCLUSION

Teaching first meanings can be practically applied to any situation, whether routine or novel. The examples discussed illustrate how well individual needs can be met in a small group or class context and that evaluation of recording demonstrates the progress made. For the pupils themselves, it is essential that opportunities for communication are created throughout the day. It is important for them to need to communicate and for them to see results from communicating about the environment and their effect on it.

6

An Early Communication Curriculum: Implications for Practice

Judith Coupe and Jane Jolliffe

PART I: THE EARLY COMMUNICATION CURRICULUM FRAMEWORK

Many new and exciting concepts have recently been highlighted in the area of early communication development. For these to be utilised and implemented effectively, a cohesive curriculum framework is essential. It is feasible for parents, teachers, speech therapists, educational psychologists and all those who work closely with developmentally young children and adults to produce an assessment of early communicative abilities which leads to intervention. In the form of a curriculum, a document can be produced which organises the foundations of early communication into goal areas and subsequent precise statements about the communicative behaviours of the pupils, that is behavioural objectives. Once produced, this curriculum document can be utilised for assessment, programme planning, recording and evaluation (APRE; Coupe, 1986). In this way the needs of an individual pupil can be identified and appropriate intervention strategies implemented and monitored.

The curriculum document:

1. Aims

Any school or centre for education or training should have a strong philosophy which documents its aims. The purpose of this philosophy should encompass a statement such as:

First to enlarge a child's knowledge, experience and imaginative understanding and thus his awareness of moral values and capacity for enjoyment; and secondly, to enable him to enter the world after formal education is over as an active participant in society and a responsible contributor to it, capable of achieving as much independence as possible (DES/Warnock, 1978).

Although essentially unattainable, a statement such as this provides a clear direction of purpose. From it a collection of core areas can be determined which highlight the main areas of development and experience. Still in the form of aims, these core areas should provide the direction and justification for the education which pupils subsequently receive. Early communication is just one area of the total curriculum. The core areas will encompass the essential areas of development and be very much concerned with the acquisition of skills. In addition, a range of experience areas can be identified which reflect the generalisation and application of existing skills as well as areas of development which are harder to influence such as personality, aesthetic and moral development. Aims, therefore, provide the direction for subsequent teaching and are a fundamental part of the education process. (See Figure 6.1.)

Figure 6.1

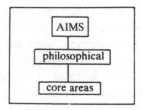

2. Goals

Goals provide an important bridge between a core area and subsequent precise statements about the pupil's behaviours and objectives. So that for the core area of communication, the goals will incorporate, amongst others: affective communication, turn taking, joint attention, vocal production, vocal imitation and first meanings. Goals are a necessary and logical break down of core areas of development and experience. (See Figure 6.2.)

93

Figure 6.2

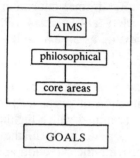

3. Objectives

Because they will be used for assessment and programme planning, objectives should be descriptions of behaviours which identify the end product of learning. Objectives need to be precise statements which refer to any child. For instance, in the core area of Early Communication, level 3: Proactive Level, under the goal of Affective Communication, one objective might be: 'The pupil's repertoire of behaviour during efforts to act on the environment are reliably interpretable by adults as a signal to convey "want".' In the core area of Early Communication, level 5: Conventional Level, under the goal of First Meanings, one objective might be: 'Will communicate the concept of non-existence using a combination of look, vocalisation, gesture, sign and word'. In this same goal area another objective might be: 'Will communicate a sequence of three first meaning concepts'. Built into the document at this stage should be clear guidelines for assessment and an indication of appropriate strategies for intervention. (See Figure 6.3.)

Intervention: APRE

Only when the curriculum document is established can the process of intervention be truly effective. In this chapter we are directly concerned with the drawing up of that part of the curriculum which identifies the goals and objectives relevant to the foundation core area of Early Communication, that is the 'what!' It remains to define the 'how'. The advantage of this

Figure 6.3

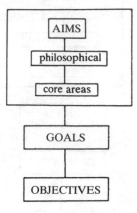

type of objective-based curriculum framework is that it is an assessment device which can be used to evaluate and guide teaching. 'Through the process of Assessment, Programme Planning, Recording and Evaluation it implies clear specification of behavioural objectives which are appropriately broken down further and provides a medium through which recording and evaluation occur' (Coupe, 1986).

Assessment

How do we determine what to teach? Obviously, assessment will help to provide the answer. By assessing a pupil, it is possible to 'discover and understand the nature of the difficulties and the needs of the individual' (DES, 1983). As an integral part of the curriculum the value of assessment is that it is concerned with what pupils can do and what they need to do next. (See Figure 6.4.)

Assessment of Louise. When assessed in the goal area of affective communication, Louise was identified as consistently being interpreted to convey the four meanings of like, dislike want and reject at two levels. She is competent at level 1, Reflexive Level, where social significance can be assigned by the adult to her reflexive (signalling) responses to internal and external stimuli. Also, at level 2, the Reactive Level, social significance can be assigned by adults to her reactive behaviours — the way she reacts to events and people within her environment. Only some

95

Figure 6.4

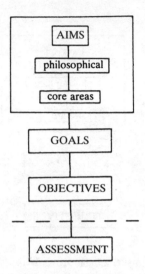

of her efforts to act on her environment at the third level, Pro-active Level, are interpreted as signals to adults who then assign communicative intent. As yet she shows no evidence of level 4 behaviours, the Primitive Level of Intentional Communication.

Assessment of Hajra.   Within the goal area of First Meanings Hajra has achieved seven objectives, using a combination of look, vocalisation, gesture, sign and word. She can now communicate and generalise her use of the semantic notions of existence, disappearance, recurrence, location, possession, agent, object and action. She is not yet competent in communicating non-existence, rejection, denial or attribute.

Programme planning

The information collated during the assessment now needs to be utilised. At this stage it is possible to identify what needs to be taught next and plan how to teach it thoroughly, systematically and successfully. (See Figure 6.5.)

Target behaviours

'Whereas the objective can apply to any child, the target behaviour is tailormade for the individual pupil and specification of criterion for success is of paramount importance' (Coupe, 1986). Target behaviours involve the selection and statement of a particular

Figure 6.5

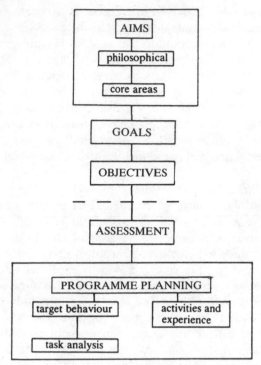

objective to suit the individual needs of a pupil. They incorporate who will do what, when, under what conditions and to what degree of success. Documentation is essential. Those working with the pupil must determine precisely what is expected at the end of teaching that could not be done before and what will be accepted as successful.

Target behaviour for Louise. The assessment of Louise demonstrated that some of her efforts to act on her environment at the proactive level have become signals to adults who then assign communicative intent. Before considering level 4, where she would be taught to signal communicative intentions to others, it will be necessary to establish consistent and general-ised competence at level 3, the proactive level. A priority target behaviour for Louise therefore will be: 'When being held by an adult in the classroom setting Louise will use a repertoire of smile and vocalisation which will be interpreted as an intention and a signal for her to 'want' the familiar adult to swing her from side to side.' Criterion for success: 9/10 occasions. (To be generalised to different locations, for instance soft play room, hall, corridor and with unfamiliar adults.) Having achieved this target behaviour, however, it cannot be assumed that Louise has reached full mastery of the objective. The pupils' repertoire of behaviours during efforts to act on the environment are reliably interpretable by adults as a signal to convey 'want'. It may be necessary to write new target behaviours incorporating different 'wants', for example adult sneezing, adult banging the surface next to her, a drink of tea, chocolate drops and so on.

Target behaviour for Hajra. For Hajra, the assessment shows that she is not yet competent in communicating non-existence, rejection, denial or attribute in a functionally appropriate context. However, the assessment clearly indicates that she understands the cognitive concept of non-existence so that, for instance, when her coat is not in its expected place she will search other locations to find it. We know from the assessment that with prompting she can use look, gesture and vocalisation to communicate about this concept of non-existence. From the objective — will communicate the concept of non-existence using a combination of look, vocalisation, gesture, sign and word — the target behaviour for Hajra will be: 'Hajra will use a combination of look, vocalisation and gesture to communicate the meaning of non-existence in the milk time situation — biscuits not in tin, straws not in box, milk bottles not in crate'. Criterion for success: five occasions for each. (To be generalised to different activities, such as dressing, cookery, dolls house, play and so on.)

Task analysis

It may be that, for some pupils, the target behaviour will prove too big a step, in which case smaller steps which may be of graded difficulty will be required. In this way the learning will be made easier and the steps will be more reasonable and realistic for the individual pupil. Not every target behaviour will require a task analysis and because no target behaviour can have a set number of task-analysed steps, how these are determined is dependent on the strengths and weaknesses of each pupil. For Louise, for instance, a task analysis was not considered to be necessary, while it was for Hajra.

Step 1: Using a combination of look, gesture and vocalisation will communicate the non-existence of biscuits when she expects them to be in the biscuit tin.

Step 2: Using a combination of look, gesture and vocalisation will communicate the non-existence of straws when she expects them to be in the box.

Step 3: Using a combination of look, gesture and vocalisation will communicate the non-existence of the milk bottles when she expects them to be in the crate.

With some task analysis it will be appropriate to teach steps in sequence, always incorporating the previous one and with each step having its own criteria. But in this instance the concept of non-existence is best taught for Hajra in a natural situation where each step identifies the non-existence of different specified materials. So that each step is not taught in isolation.

Activities and experiences

It would be difficult and unrealistic to teach at target behaviour level throughout a school day. Each child should be given the opportunity to be involved in the numerous curriculum areas which should provide essential and valuable educational experiences for generalising and learning in a less structured way. These activities and experiences will need to be drawn from an assessment of the pupil but should allow each individual to apply existing skills. Communication is obviously a continual process and opportunities should constantly be created to draw on the individual child's present level of competence. In particular, opportunities should be created to give the child something to communicate about.

Recording

Whilst teaching it is crucial that the pupil's behaviour is recorded. Recording should provide a cumulative account of the child's performance. A distinction needs to be made between inappropriate responses, incorrect responses, behaviours achieved with strong physical or verbal assistance, those achieved with minimal assistance, approximations and behaviours which are achieved spontaneously. The 0-4 numerical scoring procedure used in Education for the Developmentally Young Mentally Handicapped Child. (Foxen and McBrien, 1981) is particularly useful. However, because such behaviours as vocal production and facial expression are often quite difficult to prompt, intervention sometimes relies heavily on the adult presenting stressed, accentuated models for the pupil to imitate. Hence, any agreed consistent and precise form of documentation would be acceptable. This should be easy to use and readily interpreted by all who work with the child. (See Figure 6.6.)

Figure 6.6

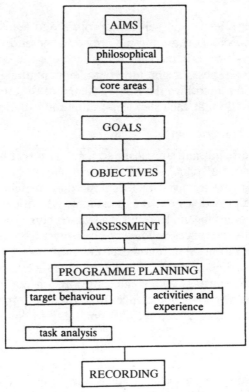

Louise. If Louise does not smile and vocalise while being held, then the beginning of the swing is carried out in an exaggerated or overemphasised way. If there is no response then more and more of the swing is given. In this way it is possible to note whether she needs a full prompt or an elicitation prompt. So a full prompt can be recorded with a 2, an elicitation prompt with a 3 and if she smiles and vocalises spontaneously, a 4 is

100

Table 6.1: Record of Louise's performance

Louise: Early Communication — Level 3: Proactive Level-Affective Communication

Target behaviour: When being held by an adult in the classroom setting Louise will use a repertoire of smile and vocalisation which will be interpreted as an initiation and a signal for her to 'want' a familiar adult to swing her from side to side. Criterion for success 9/10.

Date	Smile	Vocalisation	Date	Smile	Vocalisation
29.9.86	4	3	19.11.86	4	4
3.10.86	4	2	24.11.86	3	4
6.10.86	4	3	26.11.86	4	4
10.10.86	3	3	1.12.86	4	4
13.10.86	4	3	3.12.86	4	3
17.10.86	4	4	8.12.86	4	4
20.10.86	4	3			
24.10.86	3	4			
3.11.86	3	4			
5.11.86	4	4			
10.11.86	4	3			
12.11.86	4	4			
17.11.86	4	3			

Table 6 2: Record of Hajra's performance

Hajra: Early Communication — Level 5: Conventional Level-First Meanings

Target behaviour: Hajra will use a combination of look, vocalisation and gesture to communicate the meaning of non-existence in the milk time situation — biscuits not in tin, straws not in box, milk bottles not in crate.
Criterion for success: 5 occasions for each.

Step 1. Using a combination of look, gesture and vocalisation will communicate the non-existence of biscuits when she expects them to be in the biscuit tin.

Step 2. Using a combination of look, gesture and vocalisation will communicate the non-existence of straws when she expects them to be in the box.

Step 3. Using a combination of look, gesture and vocalisation will communicate the non-existence of the milk bottles when she expects them to be in the crate.

Date	Step 1.	Step 2.	Step 3.	Date	Step 1.	Step 2.	Step 3.
18.9.86	L.V.PG.		PL, PG, PV	26.9.86			L.G.PV.
19.9.86		L.PV.PG.	PL.PG.PV.	29.9.86			L.PG.PV.
22.9.86	L.V.PG.	L.PG.PV.		30.9.86	L.V.G.		
28.9.86	L.V.G.		L.PG.PV.				
24.9.86		L.G.PV.					
25.9.86	L.V.G.		L.PG.PV.				

scored. However, if there is no response, even after a full prompt is given then a 0 would be scored. (See Table 6.1.)

Hajra. When recording Hajra's performance for communicating non-existence it is possible to score L = look, G = gesture and V = vocalisation. Physical or verbal assistance and physical or verbal models for her to imitate will be considered to be a prompt and this will be scored by prefixing the behaviour with a P. (See Table 6.2.)

Evaluation

Regular evaluation of the child's progress is essential. In the early stages of communication progress may be slow. The evaluation will provide feedback as to the pupil's behaviours in relation to the target behaviour, including any task analysis required. If the target behaviour is achieved then the child can be reassessed and a new target set. If it has not been achieved but evaluation of the child's behaviour identifies steady progress, then continue but evaluate and perhaps consider modifying or adding new steps in the task analysis. If, however, very little or no progress has been made then it may be worth asking questions such as:

Is the target behaviour appropriate?

Was the assessment accurate enough?

Should the task analysis have been more detailed?

Are the setting conditions suitable?

Is the child sufficiently motivated?

Is there a strong enough reward?

Is the teaching preparation satisfactory?

Is the teaching style suitably sensitive?

This process of evaluation does ensure accountability. As we really cannot blame the child for failure to learn, we must be open enough to evaluate all aspects of our own intervention process (See Figure 6.7.)

Figure 6.7

Part One:
The Curriculum
Document

Part Two:
Intervention
APRE

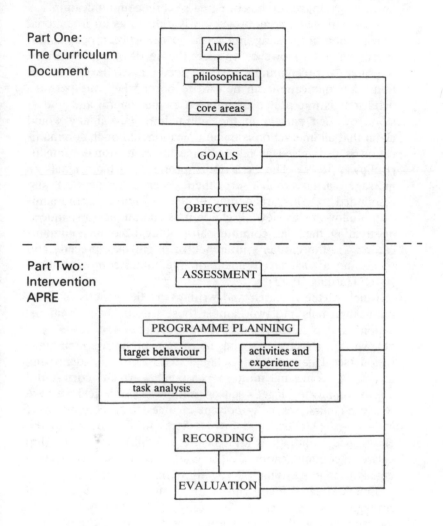

PART 2: THE COMMUNICATION CURRICULUM CONTENT

In part 1 the curriculum framework is examined in detail; Part 2 aims to focus on the content of the goal areas at each of the levels which make up the core area of early communication.

Conventionally, communication is defined as an intentional transmission of meaning in a formal code between people who share that code. However, to meet the needs of pupils defined elsewhere as precommunicative we need a more flexible definition. Communication can be said to occur when one person's behaviour is interpreted or inferred as meaningful and understood by their partner in the interaction: 'Few if any would claim that all interaction is communication, although communication is recognised as taking place in interactional contexts' (Bullowa, 1979). The behaviours produced act as signals or message carriers which are then received, processed and responded to. This broadening of the definition of communication allows us to view all children as communicators. Indeed by treating them as communicators they become communicators: '... the mother's inference of intent may precede and contribute to the development of intentional communication' (Gibb Harding, 1983).

Much of the research and writings on the genesis of communication falls into two camps: those who believe communication is dependent on cognitive advances and those who believe that affect and social interaction propagate communication (see Chapter 1 for detailed discussion). By identifying levels of communication development which correspond *approximately* to Piaget's sensori-motor stages we feel we have sensitised ourselves to important changes in 'a continuum of behaviours' (McLean and Snyder-McLean, 1985) and to the emergence of intention and meaning. Whilst the relationship between communication and cognition is, as yet, unclear, a detailed understanding of cognition may provide us with a profitable area of investigation for communicative failure and strategies for remediation. By studying the structure of early interactions and the role of affect we feel we have raised our sensitivity to the context and rules of communication and hence to possible causes of delay or failure and potential areas of intervention: '... assuming that affective forms of communication precede, influence and subsequently become integrated with linguistic (that is, cognitive) communication, disruption of early social-affective relations may be a prelude to later emotional and language disorders' (Thoman, 1981).

Our aim in producing this early communication curriculum is to synthesise all the areas covered in previous chapters and these two theoretical perspectives into goal areas from which we can derive objectives. These objectives can be used for assessment and to devise individual programmes, regardless of the nature and degree of handicap or the age of the communicatively impaired individual. The importance of early identification and teaching is highlighted by Brazelton (1979): 'If we are to improve the outcome for children who have difficulty in communication, we must identify them. Assessment of the risk for non-communication in early infancy is necessary in order to mobilise preventive efforts and programs for intervention before the neonate's problems are compounded by an environment that cannot understand him.'

The six levels of the curriculum

Level 1 — Pre-Intentional: Reflexive Level

Communicative intent and meaning are assigned by the adult to the child's very early and reflexive behaviours produced in response to internal and external stimuli. The child is receiving and orientating to input from all sensory channels.

Level 2 — Pre-Intentional: Reactive Level

Communicative intent and meaning are assigned by the adult to the child's reactive behaviours produced in response to events and people within his environment. The child is receiving and discriminating input from all sensory channels.

Level 3 — Pre-Intentional: Proactive Level

The child's efforts to act on the environment become signals to the adult who then assigns communicative intent and meaning. The child is beginning to abstract meaning from the adult's displays of affect and actions.

Level 4 — Intentional: Primitive Level

The child starts to communicate intentionally by acting on the adults and objects in her environment. These communications reflect a limited range of functions but lack clear meaning/

105

content. The child is increasingly able to comprehend non-verbal communication.

Level 5 — Intentional: Conventional Level

The child intentionally communicates a range of meanings using more conventional signals, gestures and vocalisations including jargon and protowords, which are easier to decode. The number of communicative functions conveyed increases rapidly as the child's knowledge of discourse expands. The child is now understanding linguistic input.

Level 6 — Intentional: Referential Level

The child intentionally communicates meanings/content and expresses a range of functions initially using combinations of protowords and words or signs. This makes communications easier to decode with less ambiguity and dependence on context. The child's comprehension of language continues to develop throughout this level.

Level 1 — Pre-Intentional: Reflexive Level

The individual at this level has a limited repertoire of behaviours which can be assigned intention and meaning by a mature language user. A large part of this repertoire is made up of reflexes, such as sucking, grasping, Moro (startle) and rooting, cardinal points, stepping and so on (for further information see Gordon, 1976). Other responses include cries, vegetative noises and facial 'expressions' which reflect the 'high degree of maturity of the facial neuromuscular system' (Owens, 1984). Varying states of alertness on a continuum between fully asleep and fully awake with concomitant changes in activity levels are likely to be construed as communicative. This is also true of the sensations absorbed by the caregiver from the infant, for example body temperature, smells, body contact and position. The child has the ability to fixate visually at distances of 8-10″ and to track jerkily through 180°. This early development of vision allows mutual regard to occur, 'since mutual gaze is the context for a great deal of communication in other modalities at the beginning as well as throughout life, it should be considered a very fundamental form of human communicative behaviour' (Robson, 1967).

106

These behaviours are exhibited in response to internal as much as to external stimuli, which are received through all sensory channels — visual, auditory, tactile, gustatory, olfactory and vestibular. At this level any behaviour which involves a change from a previous state and which we can differentiate, can have signal value for a caregiver. 'The possibilities for human-to-human communication are limited only by human motor and perceptual capacities' (Bullowa, 1979). In addition to producing behaviours, the child is registering input from his sensorium with particular impact from auditory and visual stimuli. The individual appears to orientate to or discriminate between different facial configurations, strange and familiar voices and speech sounds over non-speech sounds. This is illustrated by the 'neonatal synchrony of movement to adult speech' (Condon and Sander, 1974). These very early preferences have been seen as preprogramming infants for interest in and interaction with their caregivers. According to Newson (1979) infants are: 'biologically tuned to react to "person-mediated" events'. During this period not only are the infant's behaviours nonintentional but so are many of the caregiver's, as they respond instinctively to the child's output. Indeed, both partners are contributors with the baby shaping the adult's behaviour, the 'adult interactant becomes aware of his own involvement with the infant, as he too maintains an intense period of eye-to-eye, face-to-face communication' (Brazelton, 1979). Thoman (1981) summarises this process: 'Their mutual adaptation is viewed as being achieved through a continuous feedback system resulting in mutual modification of behaviours. Thus the nature of this feedback system is basically that of a communication system'.

The main messages to be interpreted at this level are like, dislike, want, reject, known and not known. These meanings can be interpreted through varying states of comfort, distress, alertness and disinterest (see Chapter 2). The content of the adult's communication is usually phatic, that is it concentrates on the relationship rather than on the caregiving activity; for example, whilst changing a nappy the adult might say 'what a good boy'. The structure of the interaction at this level has three major forms. The first, seen during feeding, is the 'burst-pause' pattern, where researchers have recorded an increase in the length of the infant's pauses during sucking, if mothers fill the pauses with actions and speech. The second is when: 'in their early dialogues, the mother imparts the child's behaviour with social significance. She provides an opportunity for the child to take a conversational or pseudo-conversational turn. Initially any child response is treated as a meaningful filling of that turn. If the child gives no response, the mother proceeds with her next conversational turn' (Owens, 1984). The above are both reciprocal patterns, but many sequences of interaction are seen as 'coactive' with mother and child acting simultaneously. It has often been suggested that this causes a conflict since, unlike reciprocity, coactions do not look like later dialogue patterns. However, Bullowa (1979) says communication as an act is continuous: 'behaviour in individual modalities may have an on-off character, e.g. mutual gaze or vocalisation or be episodic. The message may be carried in multiple channels or switch channels without interrupting communication. Once the hierarchial organisation of behaviour, interaction and communication is recognised, the problem of coaction versus reciprocity takes its place as a relatively superficial issue'.

Overall, as Brazelton (1979) says: 'We have come to feel that the newborn infant comes equipped with a series of complex behaviours for communication and for eliciting the appropriate nurturing responses from the adults around him.'

Our description of level 1 draws heavily on contemporary theories of normal infant development which we feel allow us to assess and intervene primarily with children and adults with profound and multiple handicaps.

Level 1 Profile

Sam is a six-year-old boy with microcephaly and severe learning difficulties. He is cerebral palsied with poor muscle tone. He is non-ambulant, but can sit unsupported on the floor with limited head control. Sam has poor auditory and visual functioning, being fairly unresponsive to sound and all but faces and yellow visual input. He has a range of reflexes — gag, rooting but others are absent (for instance stepping) or poor (for example, grasp). Sam's output comprises cries, whines, burps, clicks, frowns, opening and closing his eyes, body movements, particularly patting his tummy and varying states of wakefulness. He actively interacts with his environment only when prompted.

Sam's lack of movement and alertness combined with the production of behaviours which can only be interpreted as dislike or reject make it difficult for staff to interact with him. Our main concern was to capitalise on any signs which could be interpreted as like or want giving positive feedback to the staff and so prolonging interaction. A priority target behaviour was determined from the goal area of Affective Communication from the objective: 'The pupil will consistently use a simple repertoire of behaviours and/or reflexes in response to a range of stimuli which is interpreted by adults as conveying like'.

The target behaviour for Sam was: 'In response to being rocked, cuddled or bounced on a familiar adult's knee, Sam will relax his body and this will be interpreted by the adult as conveying "like".' Criterion for success: 8/10 occasions. For this to become an integral generalised part of Sam's repertoire and, for it to occur spontaneously, it may be necessary to define further target behaviours, altering the setting conditions, such as an active classroom, different people or extending the stimuli. For Sam, within this first level, it may be particularly appropriate to draw target behaviours from the goal areas of Mutual Regard and Turn-Taking. Using the objectives in each of these areas Sam's strengths and weaknesses were assessed and the following target behaviours derived: 'Given no auditory stimuli from the adult, Sam will fixate on the adult's face when it appears in the midline at a distance of 8-10" from him.' Criterion for success: 8-10 occasions. 'In response to an adult's pause in an interaction, Sam will fill his turn with any unspecified behaviour.' Criterion for success: 8/10 occasions.

Level 2 — Pre-Intentional: Reactive Level

The child is reacting to stimuli from all his or her senses and is beginning to react to objects as well as to people. For responses the child has a wider range of voluntary behaviours which can act as signals to the caregiver as her early reflexes disappear. Vocally the child still cries but gradually adds open vowels, glottals, plosives, nasals and eventually reduplicated babble. 'Sounds in the form of vocalisations appear early in the infant's development to have a major effect on the mother's behaviours and become, in fact, a focal point for much of mother's responses and activity concerning the infant' (Gibb Harding, 1983). The infant has an expanded repertoire of body and limb movements: trunk turning/orientation, whole body stiffening, changes in overall activity levels, hand-to-mouth movements, mouthing and holding. She has a variety of facial movements, for example mouth puckering and tongue movement. Of particular importance at this level is the appearance of the smile (for further information see Schaffer, 1971). In the area of visual functioning the infant is visually inspecting people and objects and giving eye contact. Mutual gaze is changing. 'At about three months, mutual gaze may be modified occasionally into gaze coupling, a turntaking interaction resembling later gaze patterns observed in mature conversation' (Jaffe, Stern and Peery, 1973).

Mothers are becoming more selective as to which behaviours they reinforce, helping to shape the child towards more sophisticated communicative behaviours, for example responding to a hand movement rather than gross body movement. 'It may be that as mothers require certain communicative behaviours before they react, they are not only encouraging those specific behaviours but also "teaching" the infant that a mutual means of communication exists' (Gibb Harding, 1983). The caregiver is still assigning intent and decoding the meanings outlined in level 1, but the content of her communication now concentrates on aspects of the caregiving activities, for instance whilst feeding, the adult might say, 'Here comes the spoon'. 'Much of this early prelinguistic dialogue occurs in specific situations, the mother attempts to divide the incoming stimuli into more readily comprehensible segments to which the child can attach meaning' (Owens' 1984).

Receptively, the child is beginning to respond more to the affective messages from her caregiver, such as tone of voice and facial expression (Trevarthan, 1979) as well as to early adult non-verbal communications notably by the end of this level line of regard, especially accompanied by vocalisation, (Bruner, 1974-5). The child's auditory responses now include searching for sound sources for eye and head movement, particularly for speech. The child's registering of speech will often produce vocalisation, paving the way for the development of vocal play and dialogues. The mother's following of the infant's line of regard and eventually the child's response to the mother's gaze direction leads to the development of shared attention. 'A great deal of work on interaction with infants during their first half considers shared attention. This is probably the key to the rhythm sharing underlying also fully elaborated interadult communication' (Bullowa, 1979).

110

During interactions the child is now likely to show antici-pation of her turn and to fill it, so whilst initiation is still in the hands of the adult the child can actively maintain the inter-action. 'The stimuli children provide not only occasion various adult responses, but they also maintain or alter adult responses. To maintain the caregiving and the social interaction of the parent, the child must produce reinforcing feedback that is contingent on the parents' behaviour' (Ramey et al., 1978). These turns are increasingly filled by vocalisation and move-ments of the head and hands rather than body movements, which is important as handling decreases sharply during these months. Interactions increase and change in nature to include rituals and game playing (Bateson, 1975), for example peek-a-boo. Daily routines such as feeding, bathing, and changing, 'provide predictable patterns of behaviour, which aid interpre-tation' (Owens 1984). This sets up a stimulus response sequence and so the child 'develops an expectation that he can change the environment or control the environment' (Owens, 1984). We have utilised this information in our assessment of Rita.

Level 2 — Profile

Rita is a ten-year-old with severe learning difficulties, micro-cephaly and hypotonic cerebral palsy. She has some head and trunk control and can side-sit unsupported despite scoliosis. Rita has limited arm and hand movement especially across the midline. She is non-ambulant and cannot move independently since she is hampered by being very overweight. Rita has good acuity and functional use of both vision and hearing, although she has a corrected squint. She responds well to sounds especially repetitions of her own noises — open vowels, laughs, 'b', 'da' and mixed sound strings. Physically she will turn her head, extend her trunk and hand but to no purpose, wave her hands and arms especially behind her head, and kick her legs in hydrotherapy. She habitually flexes both her arms and legs. Rita enjoys mutual regard, interaction especially vocal and being held, music and light stimulation. She does not like food or drinks, particularly water.

Rita reacts well to stimuli but not consistently, so a priority target behaviour was devised from the following objective in the goal area of Affective Communication: 'The pupil will consist-ently use a specified repertoire of behaviours in response to a range of stimuli which is interpreted by adults as conveying like'.

The target behaviour for Rita was: 'Rita will respond to tickles, trills, blowing and fluorescent toys with smiling and vocalisation so the staff can interpret "like"'. Criterion for success: 8/10 occasions. Other target behaviours from the goal areas of Turntaking and Auditory Perception were also devised: 'In a turntaking situation Rita will use smiles, vocalisations and hand to mouth movement in response to an adult's pause'. Crtierion for success: 8/10 occasions. 'When seated in her Rifton chair and with no visual clues Rita will turn towards a range of sounds, for instance bells, voice, musical toys, when each sound is presented in line with the left or right ear'. Criterion for success: 9/10 occasions.

Level 3 — Pre-Intentional: Proactive Level

The child is beginning to act purposefully on objects, events and people in his environment. The repertoire of behaviours, mostly occurring as a result of these actions, which can be construed as communicative by an adult, has expanded. The infant searches for and reaches for desired objects and people. He hits, shakes and explores objects and lets go of one item to examine a novel one. However, adults are increasingly selective in those behaviours they respond to and so reinforce; that is, they will place more communicative value on a vocalisation than a hand movement. During her research, Gibb Harding (1983) looked at mothers' reactions to their infants' behaviour: 'A second characteristic that was predicted to be significant in communication development was the consistent reaction of the mother to behaviours which will become communicative ... It has been hypothesised that the mother's consistent communicative reaction to behaviours such as vocalisations, looking and reaching enable the infant to identify these behaviours as first instrumental in achieving goals and then as means to communicate.' This hypothesis was confirmed by her study with particular attention being paid by mothers to eye contact accompanied by vocalisation.

At this level the vocal repertoire includes cries, screams, laughs, consonants and vowels, as before, with the addition of non-reduplicated babble. The infant vocalises to himself, especially to his reflection, people, toys, objects and pictures. Vocal productions vary in pitch, volume, stress and quality, giving emotional colouring to the voice, such as anger, eagerness, satisfaction and differing intonation patterns for example rising or questioning. Mothers and infants have dialogues of sounds with both spontaneous and imitated vocalisations from which the infant learns 'the rudiments of initiation and termination of conversation, alternation and interruption, pacing and interspersing of verbal and non-verbal elements' (Bateson, 1975). These dialogues often take place in set routines of interaction. Previously, most interaction was centred on caregiving activities and people but now the emphasis shifts towards toys and objects making the dyad of mother and child a triad of mother, child and object. Routines with joint attention and joint action allow the infant to build up expectations of what will happen next and foster his initiations of interactions. Harding and Golinkoff (1980) found that babies whose mothers shared interactional initiations with their infants were more advanced communicatively than those whose parents did not. Gibb Harding (1983) states: 'shared initiations may have a positive effect on communication development'. The infant also learns to repair and terminate both interactions and protoconversations as he is becoming a more equal partner. During these interchanges the mother increasingly talks about some person, object or event in the immediate environment, filling her turn with verbalisations and vocalisations.

The infant is more able to abstract meaning from the mother's intonation patterns, voice quality, facial expression and actions. The child now listens to sounds as well as searching for them from sources to the side and below ear level. 'During these first six months of life the infant begins to lay the foundations of one of his most highly developed areas of expertise, namely, "reading" the signal and expressions of other people's behaviours. By the end of this short period of life he will be able to discriminate most of the basic human expressive displays' (Stern, 1977).

Despite the infant's increasing skill the adult is still inferring communicative and cognitive intentionality and the same meanings and functions as at level 2. Bruner (1974-5) confirms that in his study mothers can be seen to be 'inferring the baby's intentions or other directive states'. He draws attention to two types of maternal interpretation. First, 'an interpretation of the infant's behaviour as an *intention* to carry out some *action.*' Mothers therefore facilitate this action, possibly shaping the protoimperative function. Second, an interpretation 'as trying to *find out about* something'. When the parent focuses on the object in view, usually saying, 'look' and its name, this fosters the protodeclarative function. All this information was considered when assessing Roger.

Level 3 — Profile

Roger is a 24-year-old with profound learning difficulties. At present he is ambulant only with help but gets around independently by bottom shuffling at great speed. Roger is doubly incontinent but co-operates with being toiletted. He has accurate and functional hearing and vision. Roger can finger feed or use a spoon if it is loaded for him. He is not discriminating in what he eats or drinks. Roger has few objects or people that interest him spontaneously. He responds positively to many auditory stimuli (for example speech, bells, music), some visual stimuli (for example snooker and cartoons on the television) and a variety of tactile stimuli (such as shaving foam and tickles), but he is predominantly motivated by food or drink. Despite being able to grasp and manipulate objects, hitting, shaking, feeling and exploring, Roger's most common schema is still mouthing. He also spends a considerable amount of time in self-stimulatory behaviour, such as rocking. Roger vocalises quite frequently, laughs and cries. He displays strong signs of frustration if interesting items are unavailable or out of reach, for example mugs, balls, sleigh bells, biscuits. His frustration is manifested by head banging and face thumping.

Because of this a priority target behaviour was drawn up for Roger from the following objective in the goal area of Affective Communication: 'The student's repertoire of behaviour during efforts to act on the environment is reliable and interpretable by adults as a signal to convey "want". Roger's target behaviour was: 'Roger will be interpreted as signalling "want" by moving towards a desired object when the object is in view which the adult then gives him'. Criterion for success: 8/10 in situ. Other priority target behaviours for Roger might come from the goal areas of Reception and Turn-taking, consolidating his skills at this level: 'Roger will briefly stop an action in response to an angry tone of voice from any staff member'. Criterion for success: 8/10. 'Roger will initiate a vocal dialogue with a staff member by giving eye contact and vocalising when the staff member is in close proximity'. Criterion for success: 8/10.

Level 4 — Intentional: Primitive Level

Cognitive intention, where a child acts on her environment to create a specific effect, is now established and communicative intention is developing. 'The intention to communicate will be inferred from:
(1) a context indicating that a goal desired by the child is operating, (2) the emission of some movement or sound, in which eye contact is alternated between the object and the adult, (3) the persistence of the behaviour until the inferred goal is reached, (4) consummatory behaviour confirming that the child did indeed have that goal in mind' (Bates 1976).
Level 4, therefore, represents the transition from preintentional to intentional communication. Similar radical changes are occurring in the form of the child's communications. They now comprise mainly *primitive* (McLean and Snyder-McLean, 1985) motor acts. Very common is the movement of objects for example reaching for a cup whilst looking at the adult, that is reach-for-signal (Bruner, 1978), pushing a cup off the table whilst looking at the adult, trying to manipulate a toy whilst looking at the adult, viewings its functional side, dropping, throwing or combining objects. People can also be moved or manipulated, for example, leading the adult to a desired location, putting the adult's hand onto handles, books and so on. The child can use whole body action by pulling away, co-operating, going limp, stiffening and hugging. Facial expressions are now used to communicate intentionally as are other emotional displays, such as squeals, shouts, frowns, cries and hits. Vocalisations are predominantly babble and other vocalic consonant forms. Mothers' preference for word-like sounds and vocalisations is such that Gibb Harding (1983) states 'early in development, mothers begin to selectively "teach" their infants to become word users'.

The adult needs to rely heavily on the context to understand the content and function of the communication. According to Bullowa (1979): 'Mutual attention or orientation is the context for communication based on conscious intention. Attention may be expressed by combinations of gaze, by facial expressions

115

of interest and posturally and kinesically by orienting posture and movements.' Two main functions are intentionally communicated at this level, marking the emergence of pragmatics out of social interaction. These are the protoimperative — 'the insertion of the adult as a means to attaining objects or other goals' — and the protodeclarative — 'the use of an object in giving, pointing, showing as a means to obtaining attention from the adult' (Bates, 1976). Nelson (1978) says functions are the 'central subject matter of pragmatics'. Bates also draws attention to presupposition or shared knowledge and says: 'It is suggested that presupposing is a very early activity, a process inherent in the selection of one element from an organised context to be encoded at the exclusion of other elements'. A further area is the social organisation of discourse, which incorporates turntaking skills.

Earlier we noted the emergence of sound play between mother and infant. At level 3 many of these vocalisations were simultaneous, but by 12 months there is very little overlap, (Schaffer et al, 1977) giving a more mature dialogue pattern. Receptively the infant is beginning to respond more and more to adults' non-verbal communication. She will take a proffered neutral object or a held out hand and will follow a point. The infant pauses in response to 'No!' and will, as she progresses, respond to commands incorporating situational cues and gestures, for example 'give me', 'come here', 'go away', 'sit down', 'stand up' (all in context). Moore and Meltzoff (1978) write: 'If the infant is to learn to use language meaningfully he must understand how adults use it meaningfully. This implies that until the infant understands those aspects of a situation to which an adult is referring in much the same way as the adult does, he will not be able to determine any systematic correspondence between adult words and their referents'. The infant is learning to understand cognitively these early meanings which are encoded in adults' communication, for instance existence, location, disappearance, recurrence, non-existence, agent, action and object. 'Infants learn language by first determining, independent of the language, the meanings which the speaker intends to convey to them and thereby working out the relationship between the meanings and the language' (Macnamara, 1972).

116

Level 4 — Profile

Anne is a 20-year-old with severe learning difficulties and microcephaly. She is ambulant but doubly incontinent. Anne has good audition and is slightly short sighted. Her major mode of communication is affective for example cries, frowns, smiles, but she exhibits some intentional communication when highly motivated, for example pushing objects or people away, stiffening and co-operating. She is very fond of music to listen and dance to and is discriminating in which records she likes. She also enjoys curries, rocking-chairs and the jacuzzi. Anne can self-feed with a spoon but needs her food cut up into bite-sized pieces. She has some comprehension of actions in context, that is she will place an object in another's proffered hand and responds to common situationally cued commands with gestures. She also has a few set phrases which are used non-functionally, such as 'head down', and will vocalise in response to music or speech. If Anne is not actively occupied by the staff she habitually sits down and rocks or takes her clothes off. Her priority target behaviour is drawn up from the following objective in the goal area of Intentional Communication encoding the protoimperative function: 'The student will gain the attention of an adult and use him or her to obtain a desired object'. The target behaviour for Anne was: 'Anne will gain eye contact with and lead an adult towards a visible desired object that is out of reach or which requires activating, for instance a radio. Criterion for success: 8/10. Another priority target behaviour appropriate for Anne at this level comes from the goal area of Comprehension in Context: 'Anne will take a proffered object from a known adult in response to the instruction "take it".' Criterion for success: 8/10.

Level 5 — Intentional: Conventional Level

The child is now operating on his environment in a more sophisticated way. Similarly his communication is becoming more conventional and less reliant on context or 'context-mobile' (Bruner, 1983), more precise and easily decoded by the receiver: 'The signalling becomes more conventional and can be comprehended with less contextual support' (Bruner, 1974-5). The predominant forms of communication at this level are gestures, vocalisations (such as jargon) and verbalisations (for

117

instance protowords) and early words. Gestures, that is motor acts or actions not involving physical contact with objects or people, are very common. They include nodding and shaking the head, waving, requesting (an open palm), showing (object is proffered) but not released, giving (object is proffered and released) and pointing. Novel gestures may be created by the child which repeat part of a motor act, for example a lid-opening gesture. Alternatively, the child may use objects in a way which reflects his knowledge of their function, such as giving a straw for a drink. These actions are used specifically for communication, unlike the more general use seen at level 4. Gestures are often combined with vocalisations, protowords and early words which 'are initially intention specific and may not be used referentially by children for several months thereafter' (Coggins and Carpenter, 1981). The meanings which are conveyed by the infant now expand rapidly as those notions understood cognitively at level 4 can now be communicated (see Chapter 5).

A similar broadening of functions has occurred. The following are some of the reasons for which the child might communicate: *drawing attention* to self, events, objects, people and for communication; *requesting* objects, actions, information and recurrence; *greeting, protesting, rejecting* objects, events or people; *informing* about self and the world; *responding/ acknowledging* (see Roth and Speckman 1984a, b). The central nature of pragmatic development is highlighted by Coggins and Carpenter (1981): 'during sensori-motor IV and V a child's development may be manifest more by the number of communicative intentions used than by either lexical or structural advances'. Bruner (1983) states that in the transition from prelinguistic to linguistic communication, the 'continuity of functions provides an important scaffold for the development of both referential and requestive procedures ... in certain respects, indeed, the continuity of function provides a basis for progress by substitution'.

The skills acquired during interpersonal interaction are underpinning the skills developing for conversation or discourse management. The infant has a variety of strategies that can initiate an exchange, for instance proximity, eye contact and vocalisation. The interchange can be extended over a 'question and answer' or a 'statement and reply' as the infant learns to maintain the topic and the conversation. He also has the ability to terminate a discourse by for example moving away or breaking eye contact. Of particular note are the infant's attempts to repair a breakdown in communication by repetition with emphasis, rephrasing or resorting to context (Roth and Speckman 1984a). Another aspect of pragmatics, which is achieving intentionality, is presupposition, previously mentioned as occurring as a feature of the child's attentional system (Bates, 1976). The child will actively communicate about the changing facets of their environment rather than the static which are assumed to have been processed by both or all partners. Presupposition at this level is really the act of deciding what is shared knowledge in a particular context and what is information.

As the infant's output has become more vocal, his comprehension has become more verbal. He is processing information from situationally cued words, such as 'wash your hands', said when standing next to the sink before dinner. Later the linguistic input alone is sufficient with the infants comprehending early words, for instance 'hands', 'kick', 'teddy', especially in relation to the child himself and to familiar objects.

Level 5 — Profile

Tony is a five-year-old with severe learning difficulties and a moderate conductive hearing loss, but fully functioning vision. He has Down's syndrome. Tony is fully ambulant and partially toilet trained. He is a very active and friendly child, interested in most people and events in his environment. A few of his favourite activities are music, musical instruments, wind up and mechanical toys, tickles, swings, slides and Wendy-house play and eating. Tony understands a wide range of common nouns and verbs in relation to himself and objects and can understand phrases by decoding one key word. He communicates with gestures supplemented by vocalisations and has recently said his first situation-specific word.

Tony is highly motivated to communicate but has tended to perseverate on a limited range of meanings, for instance agent and recurrence, and on particular functions, such as requests. His priority target behaviours were devised from the following objectives in the goal areas of: First Meanings — 'The child will communicate the non-existence of an expected object by gestural and vocal means', and Communicative Functions — 'The child will inform an adult about other pupils' actions by gestural and vocal means. The target behaviours for Tony were: 'Tony will communicate non-existence by a "gone" gesture in the following situations: an empty biscuit tin expected to be full; dinner aprons not in the usual cupboard; no knives and forks at the dinner table'. Criterion for success: 8/10. 'Tony will inform the adult about the following: a child finishing his crisps or drink; a child putting on the wrong clothes; a child hurting himself'. Criterion for success: 5/10 occasions.

Level 6 — Intentional: Referential

The child's progress during this level is outside the remit of this book as speech or a formalised alternative will be the main form of communication. Much has been written on the importance and implications of prelinguistic communication for the development of language and speech. For example, Bruner (1983) 'primitive "speech act" patterns may serve as a kind of matrix in which lexico-grammatical achievements can be substituted for earlier gestural or vocal procedures ... If we make the reasonable assumption that at some point the child begins to develop some primitive notion of semanticity — that patterned sounds stand for particular things or classes of things in experience — then it is no great mystery that such sounds will at first accompany ostensive referential gestures and eventually even replace them'. Bates (1976) emphasises the role of cognitive growth in the emergence of language and speech: 'The prediction is made that while illocutionary processes can take place after certain sensori-motor developments, locutionary processes for constructing and projecting propositions must await the sixth sensori-motor stage with the development of the symbolic capacity'.

This level is the final one in our hierarchy of communication development and has no finite end as children and adults continue to acquire new knowledge and competencies in form, meaning and function throughout their lives as communicators.

References

Atkinson, M. (1982) *Explorations in the study of child language development.* Cambridge University Press, Cambridge.

Barton, L. and Coupe, J. (1985) Teaching first meanings. *Mental Handicap, 13,* 67-70

Bates, E. (1976) *Language and context: the acquisition of pragmatics.* Academic Press, New York

——, Camaioni, L. and Volterra, V. (1975) The acquisition of performatives prior to speech. *Merrill-Palmer Quarterly, 21,* 205-16

Bateson, M. (1975) Mother-infant exchanges: The epigenesis of conversational interaction. In D. Aaronson and R. Rieber (eds), *Developmental Psycholinguistics and Communication Disorders.* New York Academy of Sciences, New York

Bell, I. (1985) Communication and language in mental handicap: 5: Don't teach — intervene. *Mental Handicap, 13,* 17-19

Benedict, H. (1979) Early lexical development: Comprehension and production. *Journal of Child Language, 6,* 183-200

Bennet, C. (1973) A four and a half year old as teacher of her hearing impaired sister: a case study. *Journal of Communication Disorders, 6,* 67-75

Beveridge, M. and Hurrell, P. (1980) Teachers' responses to severely mentally handicapped children's responses in the classroom. *Journal of Child Psychology and Psychiatry, 21,* 175-81

Bloom, L. (1973) *One word at a time: the use of single word utterances before speech.* Mouton, The Hague

—— and Lahey, M. (1978) *Language development and language disorders,* John Wiley, New York

Brazelton, T. (1979) Evidence of communication in neonatal behavioral assessment. In M. Bullowa (ed.) *Before speech,* Cambridge University Press, Cambridge

Bricker, W. and Bricker, D. (1974) An early language training strategy. In R. Schiefelbusch and L. Lloyd (eds), *Language perspectives: acquisition, retardation and intervention,* University Park Press, Baltimore

Bruner, J. (1974-5) From communication to language: A psychological perspective. *Cognition, 3,* 255-87

——, (1975) The ontogenesis of speech acts, *Journal of Child Language, 2,* 1-19

—— (1978) Learning how to do things with words. In J. Bruner and A. Gurton (eds), *Wolfson College lectures 1976: human growth and development.* Oxford University Press, Oxford

—— (1983) *Child's talk: learning to use language.* Oxford University press, Oxford

Bullowa, M. (1979) Introduction: prelinguistic communication: a field for scientific research. In M. Bullowa (ed), *Before speech.*

121

Cambridge University Press, Cambridge

Campbell, R.C. and Stremel-Campbell, K. (1986) Programming 'loose training' as a strategy to facilitate language generalization, *Journal of Applied Behavioral Analysis, 15,* 295-301

Carr, E., Schreibman, L. and Lovaas, O. (1975) Control of echolalic speech in autistic children, *Journal of Abnormal Child Psychology, 3,* 331-52

Chomsky, N. (1957) *Syntactic structures.* Mouton, The Hague
—— (1965) *Aspects of theory of syntax.* M.I.T. Press, Cambridge, Mass.

Cirrin, F. and Rowland, C. (1985) Communicative assessment of non-verbal youths with severe/profound mental retardation, *Mental Retardation, 23,* 52-62

Coggins, T. and Carpenter, R. (1981) The Communication Intention Inventory: a system for coding children's early intentional communication, *Applied Psycholinguistics, 2,* 235-52

Condon, W. and Sander, L. (1974) Neonate movement is synchronised with adult speech: interactional participation and language acquisition. *Science, 183,* 99-101

Coupe, J. (1981) Melland school language survey; unpublished document, Melland School, Manchester
—— (1986) The Curriculum Intervention Model (CIM). In J. Coupe and J. Porter (eds.) *The education of children with severe learning difficulties,* Croom Helm, London and New York
——, Barton, L., Barber, M., Collins, L., Levy D. and Murphy, D. (1985) *The affective communication assessment,* Manchester Education Committee, Manchester
——, and Levy, D., (1985) The object related scheme assessment procedure. *Mental Handicap, 13,* 22-4

Department of Education and Science (1978) *Special educational needs, report of the committee of enquiry into the education of handicapped children and young people (the Warnock report).* HMSO London
—— (1983) *Circular No. 8/83* HMSO, London

Dunst, C.J. (1980) *A clinical and educational manual for use with Uzgiris and Hunt scales of infant psychological development.* University Park Press, Baltimore.

Foxen, T. and McBrien, J. (1981) *Training staff in behavioural methods; trainee workbook.* Manchester University Press, Manchester

Gibb Harding, C. (1983) Setting the stage for language acquisition: Communication development in the first year. In R. Golinkoff (ed.) *The transition from prelinguistic to linguistic communication.* Laurence Erlbaum, Hillsdale N.J.

Glenn, S. (1986) People with profound retardation and multiple impairment: a developmental perspective, Paper presented to joint Mencap/RSM conference 'People with Profound Retardation and Multiple Impairments,' University of Manchester, 25th September 1986

Goldbart, J. (1985) The assessment of programmed and environmental

122

factors in teaching language to developmentally delayed children. Unpublished PhD thesis, University of Manchester

Gordon, N. (1976) *Paediatric neurology for the clinician.* Leverham Press, Leverham

Gray, B. and Fygetakis, L. (1968) Mediated language acquisition for dysphasic children. *Behavior Research and Therapy, 6,* 263-80

Greenfield, P. and Smith, J. (1976) *The structure of communication in early language development.* Academic Press, New York

Greenwald, C. and Leonard, L. (1979) Communication and sensorimotor development of Down's syndrome children. *American Journal of Mental Deficiency, 84,* 296-303

Guess, D., Keogh, W. and Sailor, W. (1978) Generalization of speech and language behavior. In R.L. Schiefelbusch (ed) *Bases of language intervention.* University Park Press, Baltimore

Haith, M. (1980) *Rules that babies look by.* Erlbaum, Hillsdale N.J.

Halle, J., Marshall, A. and Spradlin, J., (1979) Time delay: a technique to increase language use and facilitate generalization in retarded children. *Journal of Applied Behavioral Analysis, 12,* 431-9

Halliday, M. (1975) *Learning how to mean: explorations in the development of language.* Edward Arnold, London

Harding, C. and Golinkoff, R. (1980) The origins of intentional vocalizations in prelinguistic infants. *Child Development, 49,* 33-40

Hargrave, L. and Swisher, L. (1975) Modifying the verbal expression of a child with autistic behaviors. *Journal of Autism and Childhood Schizophrenia, 5,* 147-54

Harris, J. (1984a) Early language intervention programmes. *Association for Child Psychology and Psychiatry Newsletter, April 1984, 6,* 2-20

—— (1984b) Encouraging linguistic interactions between severely mentally handicapped children and teachers in special schools. *Special Education: Forward Trends, 11,* 17-24

Hedge, M. and Gierut, J. (1979) The operant training and generalization of pronouns and a verb form in a language delayed child. *Journal of Communication Disorders, 12,* pp. 74-7

Jaffe, J. Stern, D. and Peery, J. (1987) 'Conversational' coupling of gaze behavior in prelinguistic human development. *Journal of Psycholinguistic Research, 2,* 321-9

Jones, S. (1986) Assessing the functional communication skills of people with mental handicaps. Report of one-year feasibility study at St. Lawrence's Hospital, Caterham, Surrey

Kiernan, C. (1983) The use of nonvocal communication techniques with autistic individuals, *Journal of Child Psychology and Psychiatry, 24,* 339-75

—— (1984) The behavioural approach to language development, In D. Fontana (ed), *Behaviourism and learning theory in education,* Scottish Academic Press, Edinburgh

—— (1985) Communication, In A.M. Clarke, A.D.B. Clarke and J. Berg (eds). *Mental deficiency: the changing outlook* (4th edition) Methuen, London and New York

—— and Jones, M. (1985) The Heuristic Programme: a combined

case of signs and symbols with severely retarded autistic children. *Australian Journal of Human Communication Disorders, 13*, 153-68

—— and Reid, B. (1984) The use of augmentative communication systems in schools and units for autistic and aphasic children in the United Kingdom, *British Journal of Disorders of Communication, 19*, 47-61

—— and —— (1987a) *The Pre-verbal Communication Schedule (PVCS)*, N.F.E.R./Nelson, Windsor

—— and —— (1987b) *The Pre-verbal Communication Schedule (PVCS) Manual* N.F.E.R./Nelson, Windsor

——, —— and Goldbart, J. (1987) *Foundations of communication and language.* Manchester University Press, Manchester

——, —— and Jones, L. (1982) *Signs and symbols: a review of literature and use of non-vocal communication systems.* University of London Institute of Education Studies in Education, No. 11 and Heinemann, London

Knowles, W. and Masidlover, M. (1982) Derbyshire language scheme, Private Publication, Ripley, Derbyshire

Leeming, K., Swann, W., Coupe, J. and Mittler, P. (1979) *Teaching language and communication to the mentally handicapped.* Evans/Methuen Educational, London

Leonard, L. (1974) A preliminary view of generalization in language training. *Journal of Speech and Hearing Disorders, 39*, 429-33

—— (1984) Semantic considerations in early language training. In K. Ruder and M. Smith (eds.), *Developmental language intervention.* University Park Press, Baltimore

Lieven, E. (1978) Conversation between mothers and children: Individual differences and their possible implications for the study of language learning. In. N. Waterson and C. Snow (eds.), *The development of communication: social and pragmatic factors in language acquisition,* John Wiley, New York

McCartney, E. (1984) *Helping adult training centre students to communicate.* BIMH, Kidderminster

McLean, J. and Snyder-McLean, L., (1978) *A transactional approach to early language training.* Charles Merrill, Columbus, Ohio

—— and —— (1985) Developmentally early communicative behaviors among severely mentally retarded adolescents, Seminar Topic Outline, Hester Adrian Research Centre, University of Manchester.

Macnamara, J. (1972) Cognitive basis of language learning in infants. *Psychological Review, 79*, 1-13

Martin, H., McConkey, R. and Martin, S. (1984) From acquisition theories to intervention strategies, *British Journal of Communication Disorders, 19*, 3-14

Miller, J. and Chapman, R. (1984) Disorders of communication: Investigating the development of mentally retarded children. *American Journal of Mental Deficiency, 88*, 536-45

Mittler, P. and Berry, P. (1977) Demanding language, In P. Mittler (ed), *Research into practice in mental retardation, vol. II; education and training.* University Park Press, Baltimore

Moore, K. and Meltzoff, A. (1978) Object permanence, imitation and language development in infancy: toward a neo-Piagetian perspective on communicative development. In F. Minifie and L. Lloyd (eds.) *Communicative and cognitive abilities — early behavioral assessment,* University Park Press, Baltimore

Nelson, K. (1973) Structure and strategy in learning to talk. *Monographs of the Society for Research in Child Development, 38*

—— (1978) Early speech in its communicative context. In F. Minifie and L. Lloyd (eds) *Communicative and cognitive abilities — early behavioural assessment.* University Park Press, Baltimore

Newson, J. (1979) The growth of shared understandings between infant and caregiver. In M. Bullowa (ed), *Before speech.* Cambridge University Press, Cambridge.

Newton, S. (1981) Social aspects of communicative competence in mentally handicapped adolescents and non-handicapped children. Unpublished PhD thesis, University of Manchester

Owens, R. (1984) *Language development: an introduction.* Charles Merrill, Columbus, Ohio

Palermo, D. (1982) Theoretical issues in semantic development. In S. Kuczaj (ed). *Language development: Vol. 1: syntax and semantics,* Hillsdale, Erlbaum, N.J.

Piaget, J. (1952) *The origins of intelligence in children.* International Universities Press, New York

Porter, J. (1986) Beyond a simple behavioural approach. In J. Coupe and J. Porter (eds). *The education of children with severe learning difficulties.* Croom Helm, London

Pratt, M., Blumstead, D. and Raynes, N. (1976) Attendant staff speech to the institutionalized retarded: Language use as a measure of the quality of care. *Journal of Child Psychology and Psychiatry, 17,* 133-43

Prior, M., Minnes, P., Coyne, T., Golding, B., Hendy, J and McGillivary, J. (1979) Verbal interactions between staff and residents in an institution for the young mentally retarded. *Mental Retardation, 17,* 65-9

Ramey, C., Farron, D., Campbell, F., Finkelstein, N. (1978) Observation of mother-infant interaction: implications for development. In F. Minifie and L. Lloyd (eds) *Communicative and cognitive abilities — early behavioural assessment.* University Park Press, Baltimore

Robson, K. (1967) The role of eye-to-eye contact in maternal-infant attachment. *Journal of Child Psychology and Psychiatry, 8,* 13-25

Rondal, J. (1976) Maternal speech to normal and Down's syndrome children matched for mean length of utterance, Research report No. 98, Research Development and Demonstration Center in Education of Handicapped Children, University of Minnesota.

Roth, F. and Speckman, N. (1984a) Assessing the pragmatic abilities of children, Part 1: Organizational framework and assessment parameters. *Journal of Speech and Hearing Disorders, 49,* 2-11

—— and —— (1984b) Assessing the pragmatic abilities of children, Part 2: Guidelines, considerations and specific evaluation procedures, *Journal of Speech and Hearing Disorders, 49*, 12-17

Rutter, M. (1980) Language training with autistic children: How does it work and what does it achieve? In L.A. Hersov and M. Berger (eds) Language and language disorders in childhood; Supplement No. 2, *Journal of Child Psychology and Psychiatry*. Pergamon Press, Oxford

Schaffer, H., Collis, G., Parsons, G. (1977) Vocal interchange and visual regard in verbal and preverbal children. In H. Schaffer (ed) *Studies in mother-infant interaction*. Academic Press, New York

Schaffer, R. (1971) *The growth of sociability*, Penguin, Harmondsworth

Seibert, J. and Oller, D. (1981) Linguistic pragmatics and language intervention strategies. *Journal of Autism and Developmental Disorders, 11*, 75-88

Sinha, C. (1981) The role of psychological research in special education. In W. Swann (ed). *The practice of special education*. Blackwell/Open University, London

Skinner, B.F. (1957) *Verbal behavior*. Appleton-Century-Croft, New York

Slobin, D. (1971) *Psycholinguistics*. Scott Foresman, Glenview, Ill.

Snow, C. (1972) Mother's speech to children learning language. *Child Development, 43*, 549-66

Snyder-McLean, L., Solomonson, B., McLean, J. and Sack, S. (1984) Structuring joint action routines: a strategy for facilitating communication and language development in the classroom. *Seminars in Speech and Language, 5*, 213-28

Stern, D. (1977) *The first relationship*, Harvard University Press, Cambridge

Thoman, E. (1981) Affective communication as the prelude and context for language learning. In R. Schiefelbusch and D. Bricker (eds.) *Early language acquisition and intervention*. University Park Press, Baltimore

Tizard, B., Cooperman, O., Joseph, A. and Tizard, J. (1972) Environmental effects on language development: a study of young children in long stay residential nurseries. *Child Development, 43*, 337-58

Trevarthen, C. (1979) Communication and cooperation in early infancy: a description of primary intersubjectivity. In M. Bullowa (ed) *Before speech*, Cambridge University Press, Cambridge

Uzgiris, I. and Hunt, J. (1975) *Assessment in infancy*, University of Illinois Press, Urbana, Illinois

Walker, M. (1978) The Makaton vocabulary. In T. Tebbs (ed). *Ways and means*, Globe Education, Basingstoke

Zwitman, D. and Sonderman, J. (1979) A syntax programme designed to present base linguistic structures to language disordered children. *Journal of Communication Disorders, 12*, 323-35

Index